ON
BEING FREE

ON BEING FREE

Adin Steinsaltz

Selected and with a Foreword

by

Arthur Kurzweil

Jason Aronson Inc.
Northvale, New Jersey
London

The author gratefully acknowledges permission to reprint the following:

"After the Bright Light of Revelation: A Conversation with Rabbi Adin Steinsaltz." Reprinted from *Parabola*, The Magazine of Myth and Tradition, Vol. XIV, No. 2 (Summer 1989).

"The Command Is to Hear: An Interview with Rabbi Adin Steinsaltz." Reprinted from *Parabola*, The Magazine of Myth and Tradition, Vol. XIX, No. 1 (Spring 1994).

This book was set in 12 pt. Bookman by Alpha Graphics of Pittsfield, New Hampshire, and printed by Haddon Craftsmen in Scranton, Pennsylvania.

10 9 8 7 6 5 4 3 2 1

Library of Congress Cataloging-in-Publication Data

Steinsaltz, Adin.
[Selections. English. 1995]
On being free / Adin Steinsaltz ; selected and with a foreword by Arthur Kurzweil.
p. cm.
ISBN 1-56821-327-1
1. Judaism. 2. Jewish meditations. 3. Bible. O.T. Five Scrolls—Meditations. I. Kurzweil, Arthur. II. Title.
BM45.S798213 1995
296.3—dc20 94-31951
CIP

Manufactured in the United States of America. Jason Aronson Inc. offers books and cassettes. For information and catalog write to Jason Aronson Inc., 230 Livingston Street, Northvale, New Jersey 07647.

This book is dedicated as a gift of love to my family.

Martin—as my partner and my friend
we have shared a life
rooted in Torah and filled with love and joy.
May we continue on this journey always.

Naomi and Annie—I pray that our Jewish heritage
will nourish your minds, enrich your hearts,
and allow your souls to soar.

and

Rabbi Steinsaltz—thank you for sharing
the treasure of Jewish knowledge with us.

Heidi Damsky
Birmingham, Alabama

Contents

III

IV

V

VI

VII

Foreword

The extraordinary chasidic master Menachem Mendel of Kotzk, known as the Kotzker Rebbe, when commenting on the holy day of Shavuot, taught, "The festival of Shavuot is also called 'The Time of the Giving of the Torah.' Why isn't this day called 'The Time of the Receiving of the Torah'?" The Kotzker Rebbe responded to his own question: "Because on that day only the giving occurred, whereas our receiving of the Torah is taking place each and every day." The great rabbi then added, "Also, the Torah was given to all Jews alike, without distinction between one person and another. On the other hand, the Torah is received by each person differently, each according to his perception and level of understanding."

In our generation, we are blessed with a teacher whose life is devoted to helping the remnant of Israel receive the Torah "each and every day." Rabbi Adin Steinsaltz of Jerusalem, through his many writings and activities, has enabled countless Jews, who otherwise would have little if any ability or opportunity, to encounter our sacred texts and to be nourished by the wisdom of the sages. His motto, "Let my people know," is not just a cute twist on a well-known phrase; it is a prescription for health, an urgent goal for a people who have been tragically cut off from its roots.

Throughout the world there are so many individuals who are grateful to Rabbi Steinsaltz for his efforts on their behalf. His Hebrew translation and commentary on the Talmud, now appearing in English, Russian, and French as well, have enabled large numbers of Jews who otherwise would not be able to encounter the text to do so. Rabbi Steinsaltz's writings on a wide variety of subjects, including Jewish theology, chasidic thought, the Bible, the Talmud, and mysticism, have also had a profound impact on their readers.

In 1987, I found that I had accumulated a substantial collection of writings by Rabbi Steinsaltz that had appeared in various publications over several decades. I asked their author if I could bring them together as a book, based on my knowledge that so many people have come to rely on Rabbi Adin Steinsaltz as their spiritual guide and mentor and would therefore be eager to have access to these otherwise unavailable essays and interviews. The result was *The Strife of the Spirit* (Northvale, NJ: Jason Aronson, 1988).

My search for still more of Rabbi Steinsaltz's work has continued over the years. I learned about essays written decades ago as well as some recent discourses and interviews that did not receive the wide distribution they deserve. At a certain point, as with *The Strife of the Spirit*, I felt that I was able to arrange the writings in an order that would be useful to the reader. The result is the present volume,

On Being Free. The contents of this volume were not written by Rabbi Steinsaltz for publication in one book. They were written in a variety of literary styles, for diverse audiences. But I am confident that, as with the contents of *The Strife of the Spirit*, the essays, discourses, and interviews contained in this volume form a collection that is nourishing, uplifting, and inspiring. In this generation, many Jews are in urgent need of a teacher who is an authentic representative of Jewish tradition. We also need a teacher who offers a sense of wholeness regarding Jewish life.

Rabbi Steinsaltz has earned a reputation as a master of Talmud, of Kabbalah, and of chasidic thought, in addition to his profound depth of knowledge in so many fields, including the sciences, literature, and history. He has therefore come to occupy a unique place in the Jewish world; his ability to build bridges among people and to have a profound effect on the many diverse audiences he reaches out to has become legendary.

Special thanks are due to Pamela Roth, Margy-Ruth Davis, Ditsa Shabtai, and Marion Cino for their efforts in transforming this book from an idea into a reality.

I continue to be grateful and honored that Rabbi Steinsaltz has responded positively to this devoted student's request for access to some of his work.

Arthur Kurzweil

I

1

"The Time Is Short and the Work Is Great"

What follows is a very personal discourse on the *Mishnah* in *Pirkei Avot* 2:15: "The day is short, and the work is great, and the laborers are idle, and the wage is abundant, and the master of the house urges"—and what I have to say comes from both a personal and general perspective.

I will begin with the personal aspect. That "the day is short" is a discovery which I make daily. I wake up in the morning, and within a very short time I discover that it is midnight or 2:00 A.M. And I wonder: What has happened to this day? Where did it evaporate to? Every Rosh Hashanah I regret that there is no double leap year, with a second month of *Elul*. Had there been a second *Elul*, I might have been able to finish something before Rosh Hashanah. But there is no second *Elul*, and again I feel that I am short of so much time. The day is short, amazingly short, and it ends in tremendous speed; and thus go by weeks and months and years.

"And the work is great," too, and for some reason it does not seem to diminish as I keep working at it. And I can attest that the other paragraphs of the *Mishnah* also hold true for me. This is my private share of these things.

But in addition to the subjective "short day" of an individual's life there is also the objective "short day." In the past, this was not so very obvious, but now everyone sees how the day is not only short, but also is becoming shorter and shorter. Processes that we assessed would take dozens of years or more are now taking place within an exceedingly short time and the world is shaking and changing speedily.

I would, however, like to focus on *our* day, the Jewish day. The entire world is agitated and is changing, but for us as a people, as an entity, it seems that not only the day, but our entire life, is becoming shorter and shorter. I will only mention the world's three major Jewish communities.

First, the Jewish communities in the Western world. Recently published statistics, pointing to the very high rate of intermarriage in these communities, have created an unjustified shock, since the writing has been on the wall for quite a while. What is happening today in the Western world is not as dramatic and catastrophic as the events we underwent a few decades ago; still, it may be considered a sort of self-inflicted holocaust.

It seems that the Jewish people has chosen a method of self-destruction somewhat reminiscent of an ancient Roman custom. How did people commit suicide in ancient Rome? A person would get inside a warm bath and cut his own veins; then he would sit there and bleed quietly, peacefully, unto death. This is what is happening to the Jewish people nowadays; there is a constant bleeding, not dramatic, but ongoing and unceasing.

In the former U.S.S.R., on the other hand, there is a Jewish community of an as yet unknown size. This community, which was forced to be ignorant, is consequently very vague in its relation to its Jewish identity and consciousness. The majority of these Jews have no knowledge of, and hardly any contact with, Judaism. A forceful, wide-ranging effort may change the situation dramatically, so that Jewish schools of every level and communal cultural life may reemerge there.

This part of the Jewish people is now at a crucial juncture in its history. It may now either assimilate very fast—or be revived to a semblance of its former glory. At present, it does not as yet have a clear idea about its future, and therefore also no direction. In the course of a very few years, things will become set, but for now things may still change dramatically.

The third Jewish community is the one living in the State of Israel. People think that Israel's problem is whether or not there will be a Palestinian state. I think that the much more serious problem is whether there will be a Jewish state—and I am not talking about the question of security.

I wish to mention another historical point that should be remembered. At present it is rather difficult to have intermarriage in Israel for the simple reason that there are no available candidates. However, there is a difference between intermarriage and assimilation. Assimilation, unlike intermarriage, does not depend upon the physical presence of strangers: it can happen *in situ*. And we here in Israel can undergo the very same processes as the Jewish communities around us. There is nothing here in Israel that, in and of itself, sustains Jewish existence in a significant and meaningful way. One small example that reflects this is to be found in the daily newspapers of last Yom Kippur Eve. These newspapers dealt with every conceivable subject, and mainly wrote a lot about the war that had broken out twenty years ago. Not one of them, however, mentioned that in addition to the fact that there was a war, the day also happened to be Yom Kippur.

Some 2,000 years ago we were in a very similar situation, whereby almost all of us became "Palestinians." Jews were living in the Land of Israel in relative independence when they assimilated into the then-dominant Greek culture. And just as not all the Hellenists prior to Judah the Maccabee were well versed in Aristotle or read Hesiod, so the assimilators of today do not all read Shakespeare or listen to Beethoven; rather, there is an assimilation to Michael Jackson or Madonna. And this is as easy to do as it was to go to the Jerusalem stadium some 2,000 years ago. The late Israeli president Yitzhak Ben-Zvi used to say that there is more Jewish blood in the veins of the Palestinian Arabs than in many Jewish communities, and he had a point. For the Jews in the Land of Israel disappeared not because they were all slaughtered, but because there was internal assimilation.

To wit: assimilation is not necessarily a Diaspora-related phenomenon, but rather it has to do with the question of the frame of reference of the people as a whole, and every individual in it. Indeed, one of the most frightening things is that Israel cannot serve as an enduring refuge, that we cannot promise a Jew in the Diaspora, "Come here, and your continuation will be ensured."

All these things are happening now in front of our very eyes. As I said, nothing dramatic is taking place, but the time in which things may still change is getting shorter and shorter. When a gap of one generation is created, it is so much more difficult to renew the ties. Years ago, I used to travel a lot to *kibbutzim* throughout Israel, and in a few places I would say: If you do not change, your sons will not be able to do *teshuvah*: they will have to convert. And this holds true for all the Jewish communities throughout the world. We are now living in a generation in which the shortness of time can be seen not in the perspective of hundreds of years, but rather in dozens of years, perhaps even one generation, in the course of which the old ties will come undone, nostalgia will cease to have an effect, and much will get lost.

This feeling that "time is short" is what spurs me on in whatever I do, and in my attempts to "infect" others with the feeling of how short time is, and how it is becoming shorter and shorter. People criticize me, saying that I do too many different things. But in fact, I am doing one thing only—I am trying to be a partner in what it says in one of the prayers: "O Guardian of Israel, protect the remnant of Israel: . . . those who proclaim '*Shema Yisrael*'—'Hear O Israel.'" I want to ensure that the existence of the Jewish people be a meaningful one, in which "*Shema Yisrael*" can continue to be said. This may not be a great dream, but there is enough work here for an entire generation. And I can see not only the agitation and the constant changes that are happening in the world in general, and in the Jewish world in particular, but also the lack of awareness of how short time is, and what a great difference the work of a few years can make now.

"And the work is great." There is great work not only in the writing of one more Talmud volume. When I deal with the Talmud, or build the Mekor Chaim educational institutions in Jerusalem, or go to Russia for the same purpose, I am in fact doing one and the same thing: I am trying to preserve the possibility that the remnant of Israel not be lost—not only externally but also internally. And in order that the remnants of Israel not be lost, we must keep the channels open for all of Israel, so that it will remain possible to communicate, to talk and to understand, so that the words will still have an echo in the listener's heart.

"The day is short and the work is great," because it is

not just the writing of one more book or another commentary, not just one more item on one's *curriculum vitae*. The work is great because one must see the Jewish people in its entirety, not merely as this or that group within it. The Jewish people still has a large mass with its own power of inertia. To take this mass and effect a significant change in it is "a great work," which is not done by one man, or even by a group of individuals. I know only little of what is going on among those who may be termed remote Jews, from Australia to Rio de Janeiro to Jerusalem—for here, too, we have remote Jews, who are as estranged and distant as those living on the other side of the globe.

The task is tremendous "and the laborers are idle." This is, of course, also a personal confession: I always feel myself to be assaulted by idleness, not doing all that I should or could do. But beyond this, the Book of Proverbs (Proverbs 24:30–31) describes the idle person: "I went by the field of a lazy man, and by the vineyard of a man void of understanding, and lo, it was all grown over with thorns, and nettles had covered it over, and its stone wall was broken down."

The idle man does not necessarily work less than the one who is not lazy, but the idle person sleeps when he ought to be awake, at the critical hours of work. To weed a field before the thorns are man-high is relatively easy; fighting a field overgrown with brambles is much more difficult, and not always effective. It is easy to make firm a loose stone in a built fence, but if one waits until the fence has completely fallen down, then to rebuild it is much more difficult.

Indeed, the following verse in the same chapter (Proverbs 24:33) says: "A little sleep, a little slumber, a little folding of the hands to lie down." The world is full of good, well-intentioned people who will, eventually, reach the same conclusions and act accordingly; but "the laborers are idle." They rest at the critical moment, and when they suddenly realize where things are, they feel shocked, and a great confusion begins, with people running to and fro trying to salvage what they can. Such things are not new; they have happened in the past.

Laborers who are not idle do not have to work harder, but they must work at the right time. These are pregnant times throughout the world. Just as in geology we have breaking lines between huge blocks of earth, so today we are at the juncture between great blocks of time. This is a place of storm and volcano—and of becoming. In today's reality, a small act can have far-reaching consequences, beyond imagination, whereas things that will be done five or ten years from today will be so much less effective. This is precisely the meaning of "pregnant times": anything can be born. And this is exactly the time when one must not sleep.

"And the wage is abundant." I do not know the rewards given in heaven, but whoever has succeeded in doing something in these areas knows that even the reward of an individual person is infinite. I have had, a number of times, the privilege of seeing how a fleeting, sometimes accidental meeting with a person creates something like a candle that is lit up. This is one of those "things which are immeasurable" (*Mishnah*, *Pe'ah* 1:1).

One illustration: I once wrote a little book; I wrote it, and I meant well. One day a man came to me with a story. He had gotten the book and had read it over and over again, and as a consequence had reached an odd decision. He had an autistic daughter, and he realized that he had treated her improperly. So he took her out of the institution where he had put her, and brought her back home, even though there was no likelihood for him to create any kind of contact with her. He claimed that I taught him what to do. And there he was, with his daughter who was speaking, communicating and functioning—and he came to me to say thank you. I, of course, had no idea that I had done that. I am telling this story only for one purpose: to show how great is the reward. A person does a small thing and its fruits, and the fruits of those fruits, are unimaginable.

And, in addition to all of this, "the Master of the House is urging." There is a Master in the house, and He asks questions, and I feel that He is urging me.

At the beginning of the Book of Genesis—which is "the book of the generations of Man" (Genesis 5:1) and of the essence of man—there are two questions, both asked by God. The first question is directed to Adam: "Where are you?" (Genesis 2:9). This is a basic, universal question, which pertains to all human beings at all times: "Where are you," where are you in the world? Not once, man is constrained to reply—"I heard your voice in the garden and I was afraid, because I was naked; and I hid myself" (Genesis 5:10). This is a very personal question, which every man hears at one point or another, either overtly or secretly, someone knocking at his heart's doors. But later on, there is a second question in the Book of Genesis: "Where is . . . your brother?" (Genesis 4:9)—where is he? Indeed, it is a part of the world's shame when one answers: "Am I my brother's keeper?" (Genesis 4:9).

So "the Master of the House urges," and He asks, "Where is your brother?" Where is he? What is he doing? What have you done with him? And I must be responsible, I can never evade the issue and respond, "Am I my brother's keeper?"

I conclude here. I do not want to deliver a sermon that would be written somewhere in heaven. Or, in the words of the Kotsker Rebbe: "Other rabbis want to speak so that their words can reach the sky; I want to speak so that my words will reach the stomach"—*in pupik arein*, as he said in Yiddish. I do not want to offer sparkling words about Torah and *Halakhah* or mysticism, or about what can and has been done, but rather to infect all of you with the feeling that time is so short, and the work is so great, and how can anyone be idle, how can anyone say, "I am not trying to do something."

II

2

On Being Free

On the *Seder* night we are confronted with a wealth of forms, symbols, complicated customs and rituals, and several different phases of Jewish history. At the root of all this richness and variety, however, lies one central idea that binds the *Seder*'s disparate parts into a single whole: "Once we were slaves—now we are free."

On the night of Passover, this idea of freedom is given full expression in the *Haggadah*: in ritual and symbolic acts, in poetry, and in the overall atmosphere of the evening. The *Haggadah* is not a philosophical treatise, yet ideas of great profundity are expressed in its most uncomplicated forms, through simple words and actions. The significance of these acts is bold and striking, making its way, consciously or not, into the souls of those who participate in them.

Freedom and slavery appear to be simple opposites, each defined as the absence of the other: slavery, the absence of freedom; freedom, the absence of slavery. But each of these terms must be understood without reference to the other.

Throwing off one's fetters does not necessarily mean that one has entered into a state of freedom. Slavery is that condition in which a person is always subject to the will of another. Freedom, on the other hand, is the ability to act upon, and carry out, one's own independent will.

The individual who lacks a will of his own does not become free once he is unshackled: he is simply a slave without a master, or, in the case of a people, those whose overlords have abandoned them. Between ceasing to be a slave and acquiring freedom, the individual must thus pass through an intermediate stage in his progress, without which he cannot become truly free—he must develop inner qualities of his own. The miracle of the Exodus was not completed with the people's departure from the house of bondage; they needed to develop to become a truly free people and not merely runaway slaves.

Their situation as they stood on the banks of the Red Sea with Pharaoh's army in hot pursuit was described by the medieval commentator Ibn Ezra: The children of Israel could not even think of putting up any sort of opposition to Pharaoh, for they had been brought up in slavery, and they were so accustomed to it that all their old subservient attitudes overcame them afresh at the sight of their former masters. Only after the entire generation that had lived in bondage had perished in the wilderness could their descendants enter the Land of Israel and establish themselves there as a free people.

In other words, the slave is doubly bound, first of all by his subjugation to another's will, and secondly by his lack of a will and a personality of his own. A person who retains his own essential character can never completely be enslaved; and, conversely, a person who has no independent self-image can never be truly free.

What we have said of the relationship between slavery and freedom is all the more true of the relationship between exile and redemption. An end to exile is not in itself sufficient to constitute redemption—something more must still take place.

The meaning of the word *exile* is not limited to a physical definition. As with slavery, the meaning and full significance of the word lies in the spiritual realm. To be in exile means that one has surrendered oneself to a set of values, relationships, and a way of life that are foreign to the individual or collective ego.

When the persecuted Jewish people went into exile, they had to change their mode of living and the ways in which they sustained themselves. Once an agricultural people, they now turned to trade and commerce; once free and independent, they were now subject to various lords; once the masters of their own way of life, they now had to sway with every passing wind.

As long as they retained their independent spiritual character, their religious principles, their internal leadership, and their distinctive way of life, the Jewish people were never truly enslaved—at least not in the spiritual dimension of their existence.

The darkness and ignorance of the Middlc Ages did nothing to damage, alter, or diminish the spiritual creativity and vitality of the exiled Jewish people. The Jew of this period was persecuted, humiliated, and despised; he had to admit to being weak and helpless in many areas of his life. Nevertheless, his exile was never really complete, for he did not see himself as being contemptible, nor did he consider himself inferior to anyone else. As long as he kept his own essential character, his spiritual world was not merely a comfort to him. It was truly his home, and in this dimension of his life, the exile did not exist.

Paradoxically, it was assimilation that made his exile complete, for when the assimilated Jew parted with his own distinctive character, he gave up the last shred of his independence. Thus, even if he had gained his freedom as an individual, he became exiled in the full sense of the word, on the national level. Now it was the external world that determined his values, character, and relationships, not only on a superficial level, but in the depths of his heart.

The real tragedy of the exile in Egypt was that the slaves gradually became more and more like their masters, thinking like them and even dreaming the same dreams. Their greatest sorrow, in fact, was that their masters would not let them fulfill the Egyptian dream. It was not enough for them to realize how much they were suffering under the harsh regime to which they were subject—they had to decide that they no longer wanted any part of it.

To change the Egyptian class structure so that they, too, might aspire to become officers and overlords would not have sufficed to liberate them from their bondage. Only when they were ready to depart not only from the physical land of Egypt but also from the conceptual world in which they had lived, when they were ready to sacrifice their devotion to Egyptian values along with that first Paschal Lamb—only then could they truly be redeemed.

In order to achieve true redemption, and not only an end to exile, it is not enough for the Jewish people to leave "the wilderness of the nations"; it must regain its own essence, its character, spirit, ways of thinking, and ways of life. Only then can it really be free. Only then will it have been redeemed.

Through all the laws and customs of the *Seder* night, what we are really emphasizing is the most important thing about ourselves: "Once we were slaves, and now we are free." As we go through the rituals and recite the *Haggadah*, and as we discuss the written text and what lies beyond it, we must bring ourselves to understand ever more deeply that we shall truly be redeemed only when we take it upon ourselves to fulfill our need to live in our own unique way—that is, when we become truly free.

3

Freedom without Content

Shavuot is in many ways the completion of the Pesah festival. Its very name, Shavuot, or Weeks, attests to the connection between the two festivals, insofar as Shavuot is not connected to a specific day of the month. It relates, in fact, to the counting of forty-nine days after Pesah. And only when this seven weeks of the counting of the *Omer* is completed is Shavuot celebrated, on the fiftieth day.

The other name of the festival—*Atzeret*—is also indicative of this special connection. It means a final festive day. And just as the festival of Sukkot has its own *atzeret* on the eighth day (Shemini Atzeret), so does Pesah have its own. However, the *atzeret* of Pesah does not fall immediately after the festival, as with Sukkot, but rather fifty days later—on the festival of Shavuot.

This link between the festivals of Pesah and Shavuot is not just formal and external: it is an expression of the intrinsic connection between them. In other words, Pesah and Shavuot is not just formal and external—it is an expression of the intrinsic connection between them. In other words, Pesah—the festival of redemption and freedom—is completed only on Shavuot, which is the festival of the giving the Torah. Thus, Pesah without Shavuot is incomplete and lacking. And in the same way, Shavuot needs Pesah in order to have a foundation in real life. The two festivals are interconnected. Whoever severs them remains with a partial entity, with only one aspect of things.

The Pesah festival symbolizes the period when our forefathers left Egypt and cast off the yoke of external bondage associated with being slaves in a foreign country. But only after the giving of the Torah did they truly become one unit—a significant entity with its own inner content, with a meaning to its being and a goal for its continued existence.

The Exodus was the casting off of the yoke of slavery. But in and of itself the Exodus did not grant freedom. Freedom is more than the mere casting off of bondage; freedom also has a positive meaning. Slavery and bondage are states in which both an individual and a nation are not free to do what their hearts desire, but are constrained to do what others tell them to do. Thus a state of freedom exists only when a person can do what he wants and can live his own life. This, of course, cannot be achieved unless he has a will of his own and an intrinsic direction to his life.

This point applies not only to human beings or to specific interpretations of the concept of freedom. It is, in fact, the elementary meaning of freedom. Freedom without an independent will has no essence and therefore makes no sense.

This notion applies not only to the complex structures of spiritual life, but to every aspect of living. For instance, it is a well-known phenomenon that animals born and raised in captivity who escape from their cages often do not know how to live in freedom. They are incapable of taking care of themselves, nor do they have the motivation. When in their cages, they look as if they are constantly striving to set themselves free, acting out of a vague instinct. When they do attain freedom, it usually takes them no more than a few days to return to the comfort of their pen, with its well-known routine and attendant—even if that attendant makes them work. And if this is true for animals, it is much truer for human beings. For to be free means to have a personality of one's own, to have a life goal of one's own, a goal that is worth striving for despite all difficulties.

Our sages express this idea succinctly in a famous saying. On the expression in the Torah "*Harut al haluhot*" (Exodus 32:16), which means "Engraved [*harut*] on the Tablets [of the Law]," the Rabbis say: "Do not read the word as *harut*, but as *herut* [freedom], for the only person who is truly free is he who occupies himself with Torah" (*Eruvin* 54a).

This paradox is the paradox of freedom itself. For he who does not occupy himself with Torah—indeed, he who does not *have* Torah—does not have a life of his own. It makes no difference whether the yoke of foreign enslavement is evident or not. For what will he do with this freedom when there is nothing he really wants for himself? He will naturally enslave himself once more to whomever will be willing to be his master and tell him what to do and how to act.

The giving of the Torah is therefore the conclusion of the process of casting off the yoke of enslavement. In Pesah we have freedom only in the negative sense. In order to acquire true freedom, we need the festival of Shavuot, the festival of the giving of the Torah, which imparts a positive content to the Jewish people.

Attaining freedom by "accepting the yoke of the Kingdom of Heaven" is not a simple or self-evident thing. A penetrating question arises, which was probably asked by those who came out of Egypt, and which continues to be asked even today: Why can other people, large and small, live their lives without Torah? And why must the people of Israel, of all nations, be exceptional in order to exist?

The answer is connected with the anomaly of the Jewish people—an anomaly that has existed since its inception as a people. It is best expressed in the words of the prophet: "Who has heard such a thing? Who has seen such things? Shall the earth be made to bring forth in one day? Or shall a nation be born in one moment?" (Isaiah 66:8). Ordinarily, the creation of a people takes many centuries, during which a joint existence slowly binds the individuals into a larger unit, which then assumes its own identity. This was not so with the Jewish people—the people of Israel was "brought forth in one day," in a one-time process. Since the beginning of its existence, its unity and unique national character have not simply stemmed from the fact that "we are here." The development of the people of Israel is not "natural." Consequently, our people cannot satisfy itself with mere existence.

The people of Israel grew as a nation on the basis of a unifying idea, and the nation's continued existence is connected with that idea. Rav Saadia Gaon said: "Our nation is a nation only in its Torah," and this saying retained its significance even in generations when most of the Jewish people did not live by the Torah. The Torah has nevertheless remained the foundation of the life of our people, because ties of identity always draw upon a common past, and this common past is imprinted with the unifying seal of the one Torah.

This uniqueness has not decreased, but has rather increased, with the establishment of the State of Israel. The state, like the Jewish people itself, was born not as the outcome of a situation that lasted for many generations before finding its expression, but as the sudden fulfillment of a wish, the realization of an idea. This unique characteristic of the state is underscored by two factors: The first is that its neighbors have largely failed to come to terms with its very existence, and the second is the fact that the state constantly attempts to (and also must) attract new immigrants.

The existential pressures on the state, which affect all those who live here (as well as those who plan to come here), make its existence look very different from that of all other nations. The people of Israel needs a qualitatively different and deeper kind of freedom than that which is required for others.

Messianic times are defined in *Halakhah* as being based on the abolition of the yoke of other nations. This can only be relevant against the background of a previous meaningful Torah existence—one that could not reach full expression under foreign rule. Without Torah, the removal of slavery does not lead to true independence; it is only the preliminary step. The festival of redemption is the beginning; redemption awaits completion by the giving of the Torah.

Shavuot is called "the time of the giving of our Torah." Of this, Rabbi Menahem Mendel of Kotsk said that the Torah was indeed given in one day; but, he added, the active receiving of Torah happens for every individual separately, when that individual decides for himself to receive the Torah.

In this sense, Shavuot, the giving of the Torah, represents a possibility and a challenge to which the people of Israel in its entirety—and every individual therein—is called upon to respond. The giving of the Torah is not a final point. Quite the opposite: It is, for the people of Israel, a point of departure toward a long and complex process that incorporates both the receiving and the fulfilling of the given Torah.

4

The First Step

Passover, the festival of the Exodus from Egypt, is imprinted on all the days of the year. Moreover, the "memory of the Exodus from Egypt" is mentioned on almost every festive occasion.

What makes the Exodus from Egypt so important?

The Jewish festivals are first and foremost historical festivals: each one is a remembrance of a certain event in Jewish history. But their essence goes far beyond that. Whenever we remember a historical event, we connect ourselves not so much with the facts, but rather with their psychological and emotional significance. If we want to understand the personal, inner meaning of a festival, we should look to its intrinsic spiritual essence. And what is more, we should see the festivals as internal events in the life of the individual, which are reflections of the collective life of the nation. This approach will open a door for us toward a wider, albeit not immediately apparent, understanding.

Our sages say: "In every generation, each person must regard himself as if he came out of Egypt." This is the key to a new understanding of the festivals: in order to relive things, we must participate spiritually in the process of our people's birth.

At first glance, it seems that the Exodus from Egypt is not nearly as important as the giving of the Torah. The Exodus is the mere deliverance of the people of Israel from slavery, whereas the giving of the Torah is the event that shaped the character of our people. In other words, the giving of the Torah is the beginning of Jewish history, whereas the Exodus from Egypt—like the stories about the patriarchs—is, in this sense, prehistory.

If we translate historical events into terms pertaining to each individual's pilgrimage toward his true goal in life—the Promised Land—then the three festivals, together with their natural/agricultural symbolism of spring (Passover), reaping (Shavuot), and harvest (Sukkot), can be seen as landmarks along that path.

The individual journey begins when a person tears himself away from the state of aimlessness. This is the first step. At this point everything is still in the embryonic stage, incomplete and undefined—the festival of spring. Clearly, at this stage one does not fully understand the significance and future consequences of the spontaneous first step into the unknown. Only later does one reach a degree of maturity and self-knowledge that gives an understanding of the road taken. This is the time of the receiving of Torah, the feast of reaping. And only long after, possibly many years later, does one reach full awareness and the ability to enjoy the good fruits. This is the tranquil hour of "the season of our joy"—the feast of harvest.

These three stages of spiritual development can be found, in various forms, in the life of every individual, as well as in the spiritual and historical course of the nation as a whole. The Exodus from Egypt is the departure from material and spiritual nothingness in the direction of a new and as yet unknown destination. The spiritual baggage at the moment of this crucial decision is almost nonexistent. At most, it is "the bread of affliction."

Only later, farther along the path chosen without knowledge, does one reach full understanding; only then are goals and aspirations formulated in fixed laws. Then a person can see things in their entirety and evolve a bird's-eye view of his way in life and what it entails. This is the hour of the giving of Torah to the entire nation, and the hour of the receiving of Torah by the individual.

The time of receiving the Torah is a time of turmoil and inner strife, despite the newly acquired spiritual and intellectual maturity. Things are forced upon us—"God forced the Mount [of Sinai] over the people of Israel like a *pail*" (*Shabbat* 88a)—and we find it difficult to absorb all of this novelty, which, however close to the heart, is as yet foreign to the spirit.

Only after a lengthy period of digestion and adjustment does one attain a sense of inner integrity, wholeness, and peace. It is then that one feels capable of harvesting the crops that have grown in the course of time, and of enjoying them in calm and happiness.

There are three points, then, in a man's path: the decision, the understanding, and the rejoicing. All are essential and important, but not equally important. Which one bears the greatest significance?

At the point of departure, the people of Israel were a nation of slaves in body, mind, and spirit. They had no spiritual content or any real goal in life. The only thing they did have was a vague sense of continuity, an obscure link with their forefathers. This is what prevented them from assimilating completely with the Egyptians, and what prepared them for what they were about to be given.

Then came the call to depart from Egypt. The very desire for freedom was a tremendous revolution in the soul of this nation of slaves; it was the awakening of the need for inner freedom that exists in the soul of every individual. And although they did not yet know God, and had no idea as to how the Exodus would in fact occur—they believed. The slaves had neither knowledge nor understanding, and yet they went out into an unknown and unmapped desert.

Such a spark of faith can enable those who possess it to overcome all dangers and obstacles. True, this path of faith is almost bereft of profound intellectual content, but it creates a link that goes much deeper than that of any other kind. It is a relationship of devotion, of inner oneness beyond perception, with the Divine.

This lightning decision, this inexplicable faith, conceals within itself the seeds of all that will in due course be revealed. This is where the relationship begins and where its character is shaped. The overt, external revelation occurs at a later stage; but the inner, essential relationship is there from the very beginning, from the very first act of faith. This is why the people of Israel were able to say, prior to the giving of Torah, "We shall do and we shall hearken" (Exodus 24:7), because their essential link with the Torah, albeit hidden, was there from the first.

The prophet Jeremiah says, "I remember in thy favor the devotion of thy youth, thy love as a bride, when thou didst go after me in the wilderness, in a land that was not sown" (Jeremiah 2:2). The memory of the basic relationship of the people with God is the memory of the decision to depart from Egypt: The young nation of Israel, inexperienced and ignorant, followed God without knowing anything about Him, about the commandments He was about to give, or about the path they were destined to take.

The essence of the Exodus, then, is in the initial, faith-motivated decision to leave the ordinary, the routine life, and to follow God. This is that all-inclusive point of departure. Prior to that there is nothing. All the rest is elaboration. This is what gives Passover—the festival of spring—its prominence among the festivals. And this is also why the month of *Nisan*, the month of spring, is the first month—the starting point, the beginning.

The Question of Jewish Identity

In the Passover *Haggadah* there is a parable about four sons, the wise, the wicked, the simple, and the one who does not know what to ask. According to one explanation, this parable refers, historically, to four Jewish generations. The first generation was wise, deeply immersed in Jewish culture and religion. Then came the generation of rebellion, which we call—though perhaps you won't accept it—wicked. The third generation is really not wicked. It does not rebel against Jewishness—because it knows so little about it; however, when the member of the third generation comes to his grandfather for the Passover *Seder*, he sees many strange things and he asks about them. He has something to ask about.

Now, the real problem comes with the fourth generation. The son of the fourth generation—where will he come, what will he see? Because he will not see anything Jewish at his grandfather's. He will not even be able to ask questions. The tragedy is that this story is about all of Jewish life in many ways. If things continue the way they are, there will be a need not only for a memorial foundation for the Jews who were killed in the Holocaust, but also for a greater memorial foundation for the Jews whom we lose through assimilation. We once lost part of our people through genocide, but at least we knew how to fight against the world's hostility. But we are as yet quite unable to deal with the world's "love" and to regain what we lose through it.

The real problem, I think, is first that we are dealing with something that we call "Jewish culture." Jewish culture and Jewishness are quite different from anything that can be defined in so many words. I am not referring to religion, because even Orthodox Jewry can be defined by a number of points of creed and deeds. But when one speaks about Jewish culture, it is much more difficult to define and clarify. One has to deal not with about two hundred points of belief or so, but with thousands of little things that create culture, that create identity. If you don't include them all, you create only an artificial image that is devoid of content.

The root of the problem is the basic inadequacy of definitions as a rule. It is impossible to define a living thing without falling into inaccuracies that can be misleading. When we try to define Judaism as something that teaches us to be progressive, to help the minority, and do good things, including loving our neighbors, and as having something to do with the State of Israel, we are confronted with the problem of trying to find, understand, and feel Jewish continuity as a culture. And no definition in four or five sentences—neither the *ikarim*, the Articles of Faith of Maimonides, nor any newer, progressive kind of definition that tries to limit Judaism in such a way—will be very useful. One can, of course, say that Judaism is a religion or a culture that has certain characteristics, but this has meaning only as a static dictionary definition. There have been many attempts to define Judaism simply—Hillel's definition, for instance. All of these are good as a beginning when one must begin with something, but knowledge of Judaism comes only with learning all the rest of it.

The problem of rediscovering Jewish identity is a problem not only in the Diaspora, but also, with some differences, in the State of Israel. The State of Israel is of course a state of Jews. But what is the meaning of their Jewishness? If Jewishness is just a matter of being born to Jewish parents or a pejorative term used only by anti-Semites, then of course all of us are and will be Jews. But if Judaism, or being Jewish, has any specific inner meaning, if it is really a definite identity, then we are losing it, albeit quite slowly, in the State of Israel and all over the world. I am not saying that even the State of Israel is not Jewish enough. When you don't know what this "being Jewish" is, when you don't feel it, don't have it in you, then you cut your communication with your past, with your present, and with other Jews, and finally you have nothing that is inherently Jewish except that undefinable something that one calls "being a Jew." Judaism has to be a living thing and a thing that is lived; otherwise it won't work.

Our real problem is that our people, especially our youth, are ignorant. Their ignorance is not a matter of not being able to pass their Hebrew, biblical, or other tests. They are ignorant because they have nothing really to do with Judaism, and therefore they cannot be interested in it. Of course in the first generation, the second generation, and the third generation of the parable I cited, there are still some memories, there is some nostalgic feeling. But the longer the chain grows, the greater is the tendency for it to break. The farther Jews move from what some call a catholic Judaism, an all-embracing Judaism, the faster Jewish continuity is broken and becomes an empty term without meaning and significance.

This process happens anywhere—in Israel and outside Israel. Of course, it takes time—maybe generations—to forget. Only a Hitler or an experience like the Holocaust can remind us of being Jewish. But then, if we wait until violent anti-Semitism reminds us that that we are Jews—it may be too late. What will these miserable people do when they are kicked out of their countries and have to try and reidentify themselves as Jews? What could that anti-Semitic Catholic priest do whom the Nazis discovered to be a Jew and sent with Jews to be killed in the Warsaw ghetto? What could he feel about Jewish identity? This is an extreme case, but it is not very different from those myriad others from Jewish families. When you take a person who has nothing Jewish in his conscious self except that he sometimes says, "I am a Jew"—an empty phrase without any inner meaning—and kick him out, remind him, "You are Jewish," again and again and again—what meaning does it have for him?

There are many Jews whose only sense of being Jewish is the sense that they are hated, that they are a persecuted minority. But when Judaism is only defined as a kick in the backside, then it's not worth continuing. The root of the problem is that Jewish education—almost all over the world—is so lacking that it almost has no meaning. To use an example from the physical sciences, there is in flight mechanics what is called a critical velocity, under which no plane will fly. In the same way there is also a critical level of Jewish knowledge under which no effective tie with Judaism will ever be reached. Below this level all attempts to teach Judaism are quite useless. Below this level the only thing a Jewish youth learns is what I heard from a Jewish student in an American university: "The only thing I learned in my Sunday school was to hate Judaism."

Of course, this reaction is understandable. Before he began his Jewish studies, this student was open-minded; he didn't know anything about Judaism and he hoped that his fathers, his rabbis, the Jewish people, would have something to say. What he learned in Sunday school was that they had nothing to say, that the only function of his learning was to preserve some useless brotherhood, and that their only distinctive activity was collecting money for the United Jewish Appeal.

Collecting money for Israel is a game, important for Israel and for Jews abroad. It is a substitute for something more. But if you don't even have the memory, what do you substitute for it? When you don't have even the basic feeling, the consciousness of being at fault, of being ignorant, why should you do anything about it? What use is trying to give money for something in which you believe less and less? The State of Israel becomes for that Jew a state like any other state. He cannot believe the State of Israel is the axis on which the world revolves. One can identify himself with the State of Israel because it is Jewish, but then he has to feel that being Jewish is in itself meaningful. When it isn't meaningful, there is also no reason for continuing a tie with the State of Israel.

When the general knowledge of the Jewish intellectual is on a university level, and his Jewish knowledge is on a grade-school level, his Jewish knowledge cannot compete and it will always cause some kind of a rift and some degree of self-contempt. Because you cannot live with an abnormal rift like this, you cannot work with it. It is not only a matter of learning Jewish studies, but also of trying to see things Jewishly—in a thousand different ways. When we speak about the Jewish myth and we discuss whether it is a good or a bad thing, this in itself shows that we accept the outlook of the world around us. Indeed, we don't look at our history and life from our own point of view, but from without, like strangers—and this is a symptom of the spiritual malady we are suffering from.

I am not saying that we are better than others; but when we say that we are different, there has to be something concrete in that difference. We have to work out some way of understanding our own history. We know that the law of entropy is found in every physical part of the world, according to which all things must run down. The world tends to a state of decreased order, meaning that everything runs down and eventually crumbles. Within the cosmos in which the law of entropy holds its sway there is also the realm of biology. And even though the biological realm is contained in the general physical-chemical laws, it includes a pulling in the opposite direction. Every living thing grows up, develops, and becomes bigger and more complicated. I am not trying to explain these contradictions, but to state the fact that while a general rule applies to most things, a particular, seemingly contradictory, rule applies to a part of them. We have to understand our special history within world history analogously. The laws of growth, development, and decay that apply to other cultures do not apply to our people. Their times of greatness—and their ideas of greatness—did not coincide with ours. Understanding this difference, and trying to identify with it, is the only way we can really know ourselves.

If there is no major change in Jewish education all over the world, *we will lose our people*. Perhaps they won't be lost entirely, but they will still be lost in numbers that no previous disaster ever caused. The only way to prevent these losses is to make in the shortest time possible major changes in Jewish education and to heighten the level of Jewish culture considerably. Most of the work done today in this field—even good work—falling below the critical level is just a wasted effort. To continue along the same lines because it is hard to change is pure folly. Doubling or trebling the effort, time, and money spent on it may be productive.

When I speak about culture, I speak about language, about history, about basic ideas of Judaism. I am not saying that this is everything—gefilte fish is also Jewish, and those who haven't eaten any have missed a Jewish experience. Of course, it is not a part of the Jewish credo. Even those who keep the 613 commandments and the *Kitzur Shulhan Arukh* do not say that gefilte fish is a part of the Jewish faith. But it is a part of the Jewish heritage just as our language—Hebrew, Yiddish, Ladino—is a part of our heritage. It has to be relearned; it has to be relived. When one comes to Jewish organizations and doesn't find any Jewish symbol, any Jewish picture—it means something. I am not speaking about great art—perhaps we have never had great art—but in a lot of Jewish homes we once had what was called a *mizrah*, something that was perhaps very crude artistically but was nevertheless Jewish, something that the Jew identified with. It is the same with names and with other things. One of the definitions is a Jew is someone whose children remain Jewish. When I think about Jews today, I ask myself: Will their background and the Jewish education they are able to give enable them to raise Jewish children?

Only a holistic kind of Jewish education that aims at creating a set of ideas, needs, mannerisms, and other elements of Jewishness has a chance at continuing the link between Jewish people and their past. Jewish scholarship is a fine thing. But a lonely Jewish scholar without an audience, without people understanding him, reading and responding to his work, is quite useless. When we create fellowships and encourage professors and support writers, we must also create the people who will appreciate their works. Some good children's books on Jewish subjects may be much more valuable than many other kinds of books.

There is an immediate need for at least some schools to provide us with what we need most: Jewishly educated leadership, and many willing Jewish teachers for every level. We need teachers, we need better textbooks, we need to create a knowledge corps who will disperse all over the Jewish world—to teach. They must teach abstract knowledge and the laws and the history and the language—the Jewish way of life. This can yet be done. We have the people and the resources, and perhaps we still have some people who know the pressing need for it. We have to re-create the Jewish audience, re-create the Jewish home. We need schools for educating Jewish leadership so that they at least should know what the needs are. We are coming to an age when even Jewish leaders don't understand Jewish jokes. And this is a very bad thing. A Jewish joke is not part of the Jewish creed, but it is a part of the Jewish heritage. And when there comes a generation that doesn't understand it, it's very bad for us.

Creating a Jewish leadership, providing opportunities for Jewish leaders, or future leaders, to learn and to study, will be a great thing. To enable people to reach a higher level of Jewish education and to relate it experientially with Judaism, making it meaningful in everyday life and events and thoughts—this I think is very important, perhaps the most important thing for our future.

III

6

Sin and Atonement

Yom Kippur (the Day of Atonement) evokes more thought and feeling than perhaps any other day in the Jewish year. Whether it is the whole nature of the experience, even if only as obscure recollections from childhood, or whether it is the special mood of the day, Yom Kippur brings out a series of deeply human as well as personal states of mind: sin, guilt, forgiveness, atonement.

In the modern world, therefore, the day makes one uneasy, recalling as it does the concept of guilt, which the permissive society of our time has been trying to root out of our lives altogether—eliminating it from law, public opinion, and even private conscience. Sin means that there is something forbidden, something intrinsically repulsive and shameful, that it is not possible, certainly not desirable, to do. If everything is permitted, then one can no longer sin. If there are no gods, there is no one against whom to transgress. And is it not essential for the life of liberty and freedom to be without gods and without sin and without the torments of contrition?

This image of a permissive world, however, is only an external, window-display idea—hardly more than an advertising slogan. For this brave new world, no less than the old social framework that it seeks to replace, is just as bound by the innumerable laws and customs that hold it together. To be sure, these laws and customs are frequently not at all like those of previous generations, although they are similar in their definiteness and restrictiveness. A person may deny Divine authority—he is given the possibility, so to speak, of removing God from His throne—but he cannot, by the very nature of his being and personality, leave the place vacant. Something must occupy the high and lofty throne—an idea, a way, a man. This is true not only of clear and obvious substitutes for God, like the Communist International with its "church" and its scriptures, the written law of Marx and Engels, and the unwritten law of Lenin and so forth, but also the many versions of the old "live and let live" or the "eat, drink, and be merry" creeds, with their own gods, vague and uncertain perhaps but not necessarily less demanding.

Historically speaking, the contemporary permissive world is an expansion or development of the humanistic outlook that usurped God and put man in His place. However, man feels uncomfortable in this lofty place; after all, he is not quite up to it. Protagoras, the Greek Sophist who maintained that man was the measure of all things, would be pleased at the way the world situation confirms his view. It may have been well enough, perhaps, to hold such a sharply divergent view in a world dominated by long-established beliefs and opinions. However, in the modern world, where man has become the measure of all things, it seems that this measure has no meaning and no objective without an external standard. What is worse, this man, who is now theoretically in the place of God, finds himself in the throes of a most severe and terrible test—what is he to do with his "all-powerful" will? For whereas the limits and boundaries stimulated exhilarating challenge and revolt, severe punishment is in store for him who succumbs to the strongest temptation of all: to be as God, to be all-powerful, to know good and evil—and to know how all this grows out of nothingness.

In a sense, man is indeed one of the gods of the existing world. His private happiness, his freedom, his doubt, the fulfillment of his desires, all these do determine the ideals, the laws, and the pattern of life of society. There is, however, much naïve faith in this worship of his free will, in the belief that all his wishes can be satisfied and that this unlimited freedom of his will, unrestrained by law, can exist side by side with an equally similar freedom of will on the part of millions of other men like himself, or, what is more decisive, that he can live in peace with himself, in harmony with all the urges, impulses, lusts, and longings of his nature. And in this he has not only feet of clay, he is not only vulnerable—he is altogether an essential contradiction, the contradiction between the creative and defined order of things—the world of *Tikkun* (correction), in the language of the Kabbalah—and that of disorder and confusion—the world of *Tohu* (chaos)—which leads to death and destruction.

And as it happens in the case of any emergent form of an artificial and fragile religion, this worship of the brave new rational man is open to the invasion of forces that for years remained as shadows on the side—the primordial gods, such as Ashtoreth and Baal. That which began as a cultured worship of the ideal of humanity, the Divine as seen in man himself, is quickly obscured by the thrust of vulgarity toward a superman ideal. This in turn rapidly crumbles into its more material and basic parts, mainly into sex—sex without feeling, concentrated even more on the physical act. There is not even any pretense at connecting it with love, or even with reproduction; it becomes an orgy of masturbation. Also there is power, no longer wrapped in a cloak of noble purpose or aspirations, but brought down to a crude urge to rule over others, to use others. And money is no longer a means to an end, but an end in itself, a goal, a vision, and dream unto itself. Even murder is not performed for a reason, but expands and becomes a sadistic pleasure and a ritualistic act of destruction.

All of these are not merely signs of decadence or expressions of a problematic social structure. They indicate the resurgence of the ancient gods; declining Western culture is restoring the gods of Canaan and the nameless gods who preceded it. The worship of sex, drugs, Mammon, and power is the cult of the ancient gods who are waking up and returning to us. And these ancient gods have one thing in common: they are devoid of pity. They know neither forgiveness nor mercy; they do not recognize the rights and privileges of past actions or of promises for the future. The modern, well-formed young woman can easily be a priestess of Ashtoreth so long as her body is suited for the role; how desperately she endeavors to prolong her period of service and become immortal—but inevitably there is no mercy, and the useless body is cast onto the rubbish heap. And there is just as little mercy on the part of Mammon. Whoever loses his money is deprived not only of wealth, but of life itself, for man now belongs to his money. So it is with all these new gods of the world, who, like the ancient Aztec gods in their relentless demand for more sacrifices, ultimately require the human sacrifice.

This absence of forgiveness in the conceptual world of today, the impossibility of penance and atonement in a world in which man is everything, cannot be ignored any longer. Considering then the idea of forgiveness—not only from its religious aspect, but also in its everyday, human meaning—it is evident that forgiveness is a complex matter of metaphysical proportions. When a human being does something wrong (in terms of any definition of right and wrong), there is something irreversible in it. It cannot be undone; one may continue and perform other sorts of actions, one may even repair one's mistakes, but it is impossible to wipe out the past. The concept of forgiveness, however, always comprises the belief in some sort of power over the past; the capacity to forgive is a possibility of wiping out what was and of relinquishing the reality of something that happened. In the physical world, with its natural laws (and to a degree, in the spiritual world as well), there is no forgiveness in this sense. It may be possible to correct things, but it is impossible to forgive. Thus, there is no "forgiveness" for an object that has fallen, just as there is not any for a scratch in the skin, or for death.

The concept of human forgiveness is derived from the basic unconscious supposition of an omniscient presence—one that rules over time itself. It implies a relationship between man and the absolute, a relation to God, Who is beyond space and time and natural law. Every request for forgiveness of past action on the part of man is a plea to awaken in him the "spark of holiness, the Divine part from above," which enables him to exist beyond the apparent limits of reality. It follows that since the Day of Atonement (Yom Hakippurim) is, by its very definition, a "day of forgiveness and indulgence," calling on men to pardon one another, it is thus the most concrete expression of piety, or the desire to be like Him. Which brings me to that which was expressed a long time ago by Rabbi Akiva: "Happy art thou, O Israel, before Whom do you purify yourselves and Who purifies you . . . *your Father in heaven*."

7

Homecoming

Most of the Jewish people are so very scattered and removed from each other that they hardly ever find a common language, or even any language that makes sense to them as Jews. This is what is called assimilation, which is basically the loss of the common heritage. We therefore have to try to reach some deeper levels of the soul, many of them bordering on the unconscious, to help us to begin talking together again, having some kind of a common language.

Jews can hardly be categorized as a nation (even though there is now an emerging Israeli nation); we cannot even be considered a religion in the ordinary sense of a religion with a message that we think should become general, that we want to sell to others. Altogether, we are a very different sort of entity.

To clarify what we are, we may start by saying that we are a family, just a family—a large one, not entirely a biological one, but basically a family. Now a family tie, sociologically speaking, is a far more basic tie than that of either a nation or a religion. To be sure, the family tie is a very primitive way of binding people, but it is probably the most stable one, and the most resistant to outside change and influence.

The concept of the Jews as a family defines us not only sociologically, but also, in a manner of speaking, theologically. In fact, we behave just like the members of a family, feeling like a family and, incidentally, fighting and hating each other as within the family, sometimes at great length—it's even dangerous for a stranger to intervene, because any outside pressure only reinforces the unity and the feeling of the family. We can easily be separated and estranged from one another, but at a certain level, we come together again as a family, that is, we feel the unity in the way we conduct ourselves, in the way that even when we do deceive ourselves about the meaning of it, we continue to behave in a certain manner.

Even though at times we may think that we have nothing in common, as happens in every normal family, we still have all kinds of ties and links that are enormously hard for us to explain. What is more, we somehow find ourselves at ease with each other; despite the occasional infighting, we are comfortable within our own family. Understandably, too, we feel a certain amount of safety in being together and we find it easier to make connections within the family. But, of course, brothers and sisters tend to get estranged. They move to different countries, adopt different accents, ways of life, ways of behavior. Nevertheless, this uniting element remains, very primitive, very hard to define, but undeniably there.

One can go so far as to say that Judaism, as a religion, is simply the way of our particular family. It is the way we do certain things. We walk and talk with God and man, like everyone else, but we have our own way of doing it. And, as in any other family, we try sometimes, when we are young, to run away, to fight our parents. Later on, we find ourselves resembling them more and more. This particular way, which is called Judaism, is in many respects the way that we as a family move together, pray, dress, eat, do a variety of things. We have our own approach to all sorts of matters. For example, in our family we don't eat certain things. This doesn't mean that we make a special claim of any kind, saying, "We are the best family there is." But as in any group of people, we may have this feeling, and nobody can blame us. Telling myself that "my father is different, my brother is different" is very human.

At a much deeper level, the notion that our people are really our family, our brothers and sisters, connected by kinship as well as lifestyle, is substantiated in the Bible, which refers to the "House of Jacob" and "The House of Israel." Judaism has the flavor of a family or a tribe, very much enlarged, but still a tribe, sharing common goals and somehow united, even if the unity is obscured by a great variety of individual expression. The connections run so very deep that we usually are not aware of them consciously, but they awaken, and sometimes it is as though we feel that the clan is calling. And then to our own surprise, we join.

This family feeling is possibly one of the main reasons why Judaism as a religion was never very active in proselytizing, just as a family would never go out into the streets to grab people to join the family. It doesn't mean that Jews feel superior or inferior. It's simply that from the very beginning it had its own rhythm and way of living. Even when members of such a family are out of the family house, when they are wandering far away, they continue the lifestyle, theologically, sociologically, behavioristically. Of course, members of the family can be severely chastised and rifts can occur between individuals and groups, but there is really no way of leaving the family. You can even hate it, but you cannot be separated from it. After some time, people, younger or older, come to the conclusion that, in fact, they can't get away from it, and therefore that it is far better to try to find the ways in which they are connected—because the connection is beyond choice. It's a matter of being born with it. And since you are stuck with it, it is far better to get to know where you came from and who you are.

For some of our people it's almost like the story of the duckling who was hatched by a hen. Often enough, our ducklings grow up in a different atmosphere. They are taught to think and act in ways that are entirely alien. Jews have adopted a lot of other cultures, national identities, and sometimes even religions. Sometimes there is a very wonderful recognition and return. Frequently, it comes as a very unpleasant discovery that "I am somehow different," that "my medium is a different medium." When a Jew finds water, so to speak, he will swim in it, even though those who raised him and taught him don't. Finding out somehow to which family one belongs is a familiar theme in literature, and in life, knowingly or unknowingly, each person begins to discover it. If the discovery comes soon enough, the person is not only able to acknowledge the fact that he belongs somewhere (at least to be buried in the right graveyard), but also to make his life, in a way, more sensible. Paradoxically, freedom comes with the acceptance of a definite framework from which one cannot move away.

To be sure, a family is usually a biological unit; the Jewish family is and isn't a biological unit. We speak about ourselves as being the children of Abraham or the children of Jacob. Surely, many of us are biologically the children of another patrimony. But, in fact, our real legacy isn't a biological one at all. Our tribe is a very different kind of tribe. To quote an old source, when we speak about the father of our family, the mother of our family, we say that the father of our family is God and the mother of our family is that which is called the communal spirit of Israel. This is not just a mystical theological statement. It is the way our family is constructed; it determines how the family behaves and feels.

When we speak about God our father, it is not just a metaphor; it is a feeling of integral belonging to the source of the family. This makes for a stronger family, of course; nevertheless, we continue to behave just like an ordinary family. Like all children, we pass through periods of admiring father and periods of fighting with father, even hating father. We can never come to the point at which we deny the existence of our father. Of course, some children may express this denial as a mark of revolt and various members of the family may react in different ways. Sometimes members of the family are very angry at such blasphemy. Sometimes they just wait for the young blood to boil down a little bit. But always, whether one hates or loves, whether one is an ardent believer or a convinced heretic, one remains his father's child.

This basic connection is what is called the Jewish religion: being a member of that family. We have our own history, but that is not the most important part of it. Most central is our relationship to the father and mother of the tribal entity to which all of us belong in one way or another. This is what makes sense to those who have remained.

There are widely dissimilar parts, a great variety of members in our rather large, distressed, and sometimes not so glorious family. How much are we aware of these connections, and how much are we aware of each other's existence? We often try, and some of us keep trying very hard, to ignore, to deny, and even to throw out of ourselves any sense of belonging to this family. On the other hand, there are many of our people who are making a conscious effort to reenter the family fold. And not necessarily is it a seeking for "God." It is often a result of long wandering and far-reaching explorations, and the feeling, which we cannot always describe, to come home.

One can point to more beautiful mansions and more exciting sites, but these can never replace the home. For like any personal roaming and wandering of individuals separated from their family, the desperate attempt to be independent only leads to a discovery that somewhere along the line, one must try to come back and find the truth of being home.

The real point of a Jewish person, then, is the recognition that "I do belong," no matter how much I might want to. It is the deepest and most important part of my being, and one that I can't cover over with opinions about language, culture, nation, or religion. Ultimately, I do belong to the family. The deeper I go into myself, the more important the past becomes. I can reject this past and I can even cut it off from myself entirely, playing roles and trying to imitate others, but that does not change what I am. And then, if I ever want to find out more about it, I follow the long way home. It is not an easy way, but it has its compensations and its own truth.

When animals brought up in a zoo are released, they sometimes do not even know whether they are wolves or deer. They have to find out who they are, what they are. It's a great discovery to learn "I am this," and to explore the right way of behavior for one's own kind. Such is the destiny of a Jewish person who has been estranged. He may find helpers or he may not. He may almost instinctively move into his natural habitat, or he may have all kinds of strange resistances that will interfere forever with his normal behavior, so that possibly it can only be corrected in a later generation. Whatever happens, such a one is at least coming to grips with the problem.

Very frequently, the process is accompanied by tragic mishaps—finding, losing, finding again. But basically it is the situation of the person who wakes up and finds out that even though he grew up somewhere in young midwest America, he really belongs to this very old family, with those strange parents, those sometimes lonely, sometimes ugly, brothers and sisters. He has to get accustomed to this idea, and then find out what to do about it.

8

Man Was Created One

The concept of the unity of mankind is treated in two basically unconnected passages in the Talmud (*Sanhedrin* 38a; *Shabbat* 31a). Both passages are aggadic, at least in their formulation. Although there are scholars who profess to know what *Aggadah* really is, I must say that after many years of study I do not quite understand what it is. I can say, however, what it is *not*: It does not deal with legalistic (halakhic) problems. It has more to do with more general topics, including spiritual and scientific issues.

The context of the quotation from *Sanhedrin* is an extended discussion on capital punishment and the selection and testimony of witnesses. Witnesses must be warned that their statements may lead to another man's death; accordingly, they must be made aware of the value of human life. The judges thus explain to the witnesses that all humanity developed from one man, that, in a certain sense, one person contains all humanity.

This notion has been promulgated in general literature, not only in Jewish sources. It can be summarized by the formula "Man was created one": one person is the end and the beginning of humanity.

Why is there a need to say this, the Talmud asks? In the first place, the statement is necessary in order to prevent heretics from saying that there are many rulers in heaven. The term *heretics* (*minim*) usually refers, not to the early Christians, but rather to several sects related to the Gnostics, who held that there was a dichotomy in heaven between Good and Evil. Man has been created one because if this were not the case, it could be said that whereas part of mankind stems from the forces of Good, part of it originated in the forces of Evil.

But other explanations are given for this statement. Had there been two pristine men, the righteous would claim descent from the righteous ancestor, and the wicked would say that they are the offspring of the wicked man. In Jewish thought each human being is considered to have more or less equal chances. There is no possible justification for good or bad action in any innate compulsion, or any absolute determinism. The righteous cannot say: "I am the son of the righteous one and therefore act, by definition, in the right way. You are the son of the wicked and therefore do evil." It is a common psychological attitude that prompts people to argue that they come from an evil background and therefore have ample justification for performing any kind of evil deed. Such arguments cannot be defended when people recognize that every human being stems from one unique origin. The righteous have no automatic assurance that they will remain good, and the wicked have no compulsory reason to continue in their ways.

A further reason that man was created one is related to genealogy: families should not fight over questions of superiority. Even after knowing that man was created one, families still argue over who is of more venerable descent. Thus, what would have happened if there had been several pristine men! This is another example of a fight for primacy and superiority. According to the sages of the Talmud, there is no justification for any man's claiming a better, nobler origin than that of any other.

The Talmud then discusses robbers and cheats. Despite the knowledge that man was created one, there are many robbers and swindlers; what would have been the case had the origin of man been multiple? This means of course that one of the possible justifications for robbing or cheating is the assertion that one's fellowman is inferior. One could say, for instance: I descend from Homo pekinensis whereas you stem only from Homo cromagnonis; therefore I have the right to rob or kill you, as we are not really of the same stock.

In the face of all the wrongs and evil deeds that are perpetrated all over the world and fill the newspapers, the notion that everyone remains a human being, and that this is a common denominator, might even serve as a corrective. Whether black, yellow, or white, all come from the same unique origin.

This approach to humanity somehow lowers the pride of those who are high up and gives some hope to those who are lower down the scale. No one can claim to have the right to harm or coerce others on the grounds that he is better.

There is a Hebrew pun with a psychological dimension that may be relevant to this discussion. The word *akhzar*, meaning cruel, can be divided into *akh* (but) and *zar* (stranger). Thus, the word itself captures the notion that cruelty is based on the inability to empathize. When the other person is no longer considered a stranger, the ability to be cruel toward him diminishes considerably. It is well known that killing someone from a distance is much easier, because the killer does not see his victim distinctly—he is an alien, a stranger. Thus it seems that there should be a sense of equality among human beings, despite all the existing differences, which cannot be denied.

The methodology of the Talmud is generally dialectical, including multiple statements, some of them complementary, others contradictory. In our case, all the statements mentioned so far go in the same direction: they aim toward stressing the unity of man's origin and countering any sense of difference, of superiority.

This leads us to a new approach. Every person, says the Talmud, contains something of the pristine man. Every human being, so to speak, is Adam himself. This statement aims to emphasize the greatness of God, "to show the greatness of the King of the King's kings" (*Melekh Malkhei HaMelakhim*). When man mints coins from one and the same mold, they are all perfectly similar. But although God makes every man according to the cast of the first man, of Adam, no one closely resembles the other.

We are witnessing here a new talmudic move. Contrary to the previous statements, which all stressed the uniqueness of man, the latter indicates that from this unique origin stems a multiplicity of forms, a differentiation of humanity. Although all men are basically equal, they are also deeply differentiated and cannot be exactly duplicated. Every human being is therefore irreplaceable. To borrow from genetic terminology, the nature of man is so plastic that, with the exception of twins, no human beings have exactly the same genetic make-up. Faces are different; minds also are different.

Why should faces be different? A talmudic statement, which appears elsewhere, declares that one could be tempted to affirm, when meeting a beautiful woman or seeing a nice house, "This is mine." Therefore personal identities are necessary, from a social point of view.

Rabbi Meir says: People are different in three ways: in their voices, faces, and *daat*. The term *daat* is very difficult to define precisely. It certainly cannot be translated as knowledge. Sometimes it means esprit and sometimes sense or sensibility. *Daat* is, in my view, the peculiar way in which a given person sees things. It might accordingly be translated as personality or, at least, the overall stamp of personality. Thus, somebody can be very clever and scholarly, while being in no way a *ben-daat*.

Although the above talmudic passage merits further analysis, two main conclusions stand out at this point. All humanity is derived from a single stock and converges into one unique individual; this has numerous sociological and political consequences. There are many individuals among the Jewish people who claim that they descend from an illustrious lineage. But they should understand that they ultimately stem from Abraham, and, before him, from his father Terah—which is not exactly a lineage that one can be particularly proud of. Therefore, one should not insist too much on pursuing questions of lineage.

At the same time, the diversity of human beings and differences among individuals are mentioned in this passage. This can be summed up in the formula: "People are equal, but not similar." People should feel that although they are different from one another, there is something within them that makes them equal.

Let us now turn to another text, *Shabbat* 31a. This passage features a story that, although apparently unrelated to the previous text, is nonetheless anthropological in nature. The story reads as follows:

Two persons made a bet: Whoever succeeds in making the sage Hillel angry will receive 400 *zuz*[1] from the other.

---

1. Four hundred *zuz* was a considerable sum of money, the equivalent of a three months' salary for an ordinary worker.

At this time, Hillel was the supreme religious authority and was famous for his piety, his wisdom, and his moral character. He was known to be very humble, and it was common knowledge that nobody had ever succeeded in enraging him.

Then, one of the two went to see Hillel at his home. It was on the eve of *Shabbat*, just at the transition between the weekday and *Shabbat*, a moment when people wish to be alone. Hillel was washing his hair, again a situation that is certainly not conducive to any kind of discussion. The man approached, knocked at the door, and shouted, "Is there a Hillel here? Is there a Hillel here?" (a salutation considered offensive in its very formulation).

Hillel immediately wrapped himself and came out. This means that he dressed himself formally in order to greet his visitor properly, without taking into account his identity, rank, or origin.

Hillel said to him, "My son, what do you want?"

He answered, "I have a question to ask."

Hillel replied, "Ask my son, ask!"

"Why are the heads of the Babylonians rounded?" the man asked. . . .

Such a question is, by its very nature, somewhat offensive (Hillel was himself of Babylonian origin); it is, moreover, quite insignificant, and was asked at a most unfitting and troublesome time. This combination was intended to make the situation as difficult and irritating as possible.

Hillel answered, "My son, you have asked an important question! The answer is: because they do not have wise midwives." This means that the Babylonian midwives do not shape the heads of newborn babies properly.

The man went away and waited for some time. Then

he returned to Hillel's house and shouted again: "Is there a Hillel here? Is there a Hillel here?"

Hillel again dressed and came out. He said, "My son, what do you want?"

"I have a question to ask," replied the man.

"Ask my son, ask," said Hillel.

"Why are the eyes of the people from Tarmod[2] runny?" asked the man.

"My son, you have asked an important question! The reason is: because they are living in a sandy area."

The man returned a third time and, after the same preliminary dialogue, asked the following question: "Why are the feet of the Africans flat?"

"My son," replied Hillel, "you asked an important question! The answer is: because they live in a swampy area."

Let me mention here a remark made several years ago by the late Dr. Even-Shemuel (Kaufman), in South Africa—a rather appropriate location! The point of this story, he remarked, is not simply to show the extreme patience and humility of Hillel, although both attributes are demonstrated in a very striking manner. The particular three questions asked by the man are not just incidental; they also convey a message. All three cases point out that people are somehow different from each other. Some have round heads, others have "running" eyes, and so forth.

By the way, another translation of the term *terutot* (running) is narrow—perhaps some kind of mongoloid shape. Others understand it to mean elongated. Scholars have suggested at least three Greek roots for *terutot*, and perhaps

---

2. Tarmod [or Tadmor] was the ancient city of Palmyra, an oasis in the Syrian desert.

none of them is entirely correct. As for the African's feet, there is indeed a notion within medical anthropology that their feet have special characteristics.

All three of these questions appear to be of a racist nature. They aim at stressing the differences between peoples. Moreover, Hillel himself was of Babylonian origin, and Babylonians—even Babylonian Jews—were not always well accepted in this country. As we know, such an attitude toward strangers is still present everywhere in modern times. Therefore these racist questions may have reflected, to a certain extent at least, a racist attitude toward Hillel himself.

But Hillel dealt with these questions in a uniform manner. To use modern phrasing, he stressed the fact that the differences existing between people are not genetic. They are acquired traits determined either by the external environment or by midwives.

To be sure, there are distinct ethnic groups, races, families, and other differentiating factors within humanity. These groups are subject to changes caused by external influences, but the differences between them are only superficial.

It may be added, by the way, that even the "racists" of talmudic times, such as the person who asked the questions, did not manifest any color prejudice. He says "the Africans," not "the blacks." Some information is available regarding the colors that were referred to in mishnaic times in such a context. There is a talmudic statement that reads: "Jews are not black like Negroes, they are not white like Germans, they are brownish like the bark of a tree." Apparently, the color of skin was not a central issue for our forefathers.

Returning to our story, Hillel was not just being ironical when he answered time after time, "My son, you have asked an important question!" Most probably, however, the importance of the questions was not evident to the man who asked them! He just wanted to be as bothersome as possible, while being unaware of the underlying implications of his questions.

Hillel's answers were in fact informed by his knowledge of the above passage of *Sanhedrin*. If mankind stems from one unique origin, all the differences characterizing races and ethnic groups are epiphenomena caused by external factors, not inborn traits.

Furthermore, historically speaking, this country (the Land of Israel) was in antiquity the crossroads of several cultures and continents, and even through the Middle Ages, there could be found more racial types here than in any other part of the world. People thus had good reason to ask such racial questions and to interrogate themselves and others about human differences.

As is usual in talmudic lore, the approach of the sages is realistic and matter-of-fact. I am not convinced that Jewish philosophy is strictly optimistic. Rather, I would say that, at least in talmudic times, the sages' optimism was limited and tempered by a realistic—perhaps even too realistic—outlook. It is therefore important to underline that the Talmud considers people prone to change and suggests that nothing is immutably fixed by heredity: human beings remain flexible.

This does not mean that there is no notion of hereditary traits in the Talmud. On the contrary, a number of diseases were considered in the Talmud to be hereditary, or at least were suspected of being hereditary. But this does not preclude the reality that people change through successive generations and can evolve in either direction, good or evil. The statement is made, therefore, that a bad son cannot be rejected or disinherited to the advantage of a good one, since no one can know what kind of descendants each will have.

Another question raised by the Talmud is: Why was it so rare that great scholars had illustrious sons or descendants? The point is that there is no guarantee of the continuation of trends. Therefore, it is of no importance and of no avail to consider one given family or race as superior to another.

Returning to the story of Hillel and his questioner, the latter added, after Hillel had answered his third question, "I have many [other] questions to ask, but I am afraid that you will become angry!"

So Hillel again wrapped himself up—which means that he dressed properly, as people in antiquity did when they had an important meeting—and sat down. He said, "My son, all the questions you wish to ask, come and ask."

The questioner said, "Are you really Hillel, the one who is called the prince, the chief of Israel [*nessi Yisrael*]?"

Hillel answered, "Yes, I am."

"If you are that one, then I wish that there would not be more like you in Israel!"

Hillel then asked, "Why so, my son?"

"Because I just lost 400 *zuz* because of you!"

"Be very careful," said the sage. "Hillel is made in such a way that you can lose 400 *zuz*, and another 400 *zuz* thanks to him, and he will not get angry."

Now Hillel is certainly not depicted here as a holy simpleton; nor is just his exemplary patience emphasized.

Hillel knew from the beginning that the visitor was trying to enrage him, and his patient replies actually succeeded in enraging his questioner!

To summarize these two passages of the Talmud, although basically unrelated, they still discuss the same problem. In this case, the sages did not deal with, or try to find the solution to, a problem; rather, they made several related statements.

Humanity is one; and with all their differences, all men are equal.

The second story, that of Hillel, begins with the idea that, while there are many different peoples and races, human beings are basically the same.

The first statement is theological: all humanity stems from the same root. The second is sociological and biological: no one can ignore the differences that obviously separate human beings.

Hillel could have answered by taking a relativistic attitude: not all the Babylonians have round heads, not all the inhabitants of Tarmod have running eyes, and so forth. But this was not the aim of the Talmud. There *are* differences within mankind, which can, and even should, be explained. To put it in another way: man was born one, and the miracle is that, derived from one source and nonetheless so different, human beings remain, existentially speaking, *one*.

IV

Modern Man and His Prayer

Many of the Jews who come to the synagogue on the holy days of Rosh Hashanah and Yom Kippur are not regular worshipers; they don't attend prayer services during the rest of the year. And no less than these are the many who would like to come but who do not have the heart to do so. Both of these kinds of Jews wonder whether it is at all possible for a contemporary person to pray. How can a modern man do such a thing?

Of course, this question is usually asked surreptitiously, being the sort of question a person puts only to himself. At times it belongs to the unspoken queries of the heart that never emerge at all but assume a certain urgency at this season of the year.

The truth is that this question has a considerable degree of naïveté about it. And naïveté does not necessarily belong only to the innocent or the unlearned. There is another kind of naïveté, that of the intellectual (both the genuine and the make-believe). A person can be very well educated, sharp and discerning in many fields, and at the same time display surprising innocence in other areas of life, especially those with which he has had little contact.

It is generally believed that in our generation, when "spiritual" persons show themselves to be sharp and clever about their financial affairs, and when sex is a commonplace and tedious subject of conversation, there is not much room for innocence and simplicity. But it is not so. Our contemporary society, which may be bringing to light areas of life that were once kept hidden, is still concealing from itself many critical aspects of mind and heart. In our time, when the mention of God's name or even thinking of Him is intellectually out of bounds for so many people, this entire realm is obscured in a mantle of secrecy and kept discreetly out of the framework of decent conversation. It is therefore hardly surprising if certain individuals seek their satisfaction elsewhere and get themselves involved with strange cults and faiths.

With all the changes and differences, the achievements, sins, and distortions of modern man (and so few are really new), he has still not transcended the basic limitations of his humanity. The fundamental problems of life today are the same as those of one thousand and three thousand years ago. There is the same wretchedness and suffering of the heart as ever. The only difference is that many people keep God out of bounds—even when they are really looking for Him everywhere.

Many people say "I don't believe," and may even be convinced of it in all sincerity. But it is not at all so simple. Heresy and atheism require that a person should at least know what he is rejecting. When the modern Jew declares, "I don't believe," he is really saying that he does not believe in the things that religious people believe in. Moreover, in most cases, what is really happening to the person is something altogether different. Most concepts of belief and of Jewishness are acquired in the kindergarten years, with perhaps occasional additions in the preparation for *bar mitzvah*. When these childish conceptions confront a man's adult knowledge, it is no wonder that they are promptly rejected as inappropriate in the declaration "I don't believe." Often enough, someone who considers himself a wicked and even sinful person is only an innocent who does not even know enough to ask the right questions.

I don't mean to imply that when a person begins to ask the right questions he will immediately believe in Maimonides' Thirteen Articles of Faith. Belief is not a simple mental procedure for anyone, and certainly not for the genuinely religious individual. A certain *tzadik* (righteous person) used to say that the opening words of the Thirteen Articles of Faith, "I believe with complete faith," are not a declaration but a prayer, the prayer for the attainment of complete faith. If a person can really shake off the mountains of dust of accumulated opinions and actions, and truly examine himself inwardly, he will find there the spark of faith that was never really extinguished.

Among those who say they have never prayed at all in their lives, there are not a few who regularly speak words of prayer at all sorts of occasions, not necessarily in the synagogue or at the set times for prayer. There is prayer of thanksgiving for the good and the beautiful, and prayer of supplication in an hour of distress and great need; there are those who pronounce the words of prayer with their lips, and those who think them in their hearts. Only very few people can do without prayer at all.

Thus the real question is: How does one pray in the synagogue, if one doesn't have any connection with the place and its worshipers, when the words do not express one's innermost feelings? To be honest, the same question in all its acuteness troubles many of the others, too, including those who pray three times a day as prescribed. How can one turn to the Divine in prayer? What do the words of prayer mean? These are not necessarily modern questions, or even specifically secular. They are the very same queries every worshiper asks in the depths of his heart. What is more, and this is the paradox of prayer, praying is itself the struggle with these questions.

The very word *tefillah* (prayer) shares the same root as *naftolin* (struggle). Prayer is a wrestling of man with the angel, the struggle of man with the Holy One, Blessed be He. *Tefillah* is also connected with *plilim* (jurisprudence); thus, prayer is a trial in which man is brought to court against himself, in which he judges his world and pleads his case with his Maker. Many of the psalms (which make up much of the recital in prayer) relate to the beauty and perfection of nature. And in addition, prayer includes words of thanksgiving and passages of complaint.

What should not be dismissed is the presence of the congregation; prayer in the synagogue is done with others even if it is a highly individual action. Every person can, and indeed should, direct his prayer as something private between himself and his Creator. But at the same time, there is a common worship within a congregation, within any Jewish community in one city or another in any country, in any time. The public prayer includes the individual in something larger—the person becomes part of a people, not only the thousands of his countrymen who are similarly engaged at that moment or on that day all over the world, but also the millions of Jews who prayed in this way throughout the generations. The place of worship embraces the whole world, past, present, and future.

Consequently, we cannot expect that the ritual prayer should fit the measure of each person in every place. Indeed, the problems of the specific generation or of the individual are scarcely hinted at in the traditional prayer, although every person can find the appropriate word, phrase, or sentence that speaks especially to him. This public worship, which is heard as a single voice, is the result of the choir of the voices of Jews of every era, in which each voice joins, according to its own pitch and tone and volume, to the general song.

There is perhaps no more satisfying description of the essence of prayer than the words of King Solomon at the inauguration of the Holy Temple (1 Kings 8:38–39): "When a prayer or supplication is uttered by any man of the House of Israel, who is aware of that which plagues his heart—if he spreads out his hands in supplication toward this house, may You hear him from the heavens, Your dwelling place, and may You forgive him and deal with each person according to his ways, because You know his heart—for indeed You alone know the heart of each person."

10

Prayer Education

The question as to whether and how it is possible to educate for prayer seems to me to lead directly to another, far more fundamental question, namely, what is the nature of prayer?

I would like to explain at the outset why I think that this is the fundamental question. An individual who prays for himself only can pray parrot-fashion, or like a professor, nor does he need to give an account either of the reason for praying or of the content of his prayer. And even if he does think about these things, he is under no obligation to account for himself to anyone else, which is not the case when he has to act as an educator. A true teacher cannot avoid a long list of complicated and painful questions regarding the nature, value, subject, and function of prayer, for the simple reason that that is what is required of him. This is the case not only for the professional educator, but for anyone who finds himself, in one way or another, called upon to inculcate in others the desire and the ability to pray.

In the same manner as this question poses itself to the teacher or educator, it is asked no less (and sometimes in a far sharper and more personal fashion) of every Jewish father who wishes that his children should pray (and there are still such fathers in the world). A father, even if he has no wish to become involved in theology, will be confronted with a pile of questions, which he will be required to clarify, at least to his own satisfaction, as to what he is doing and what he has in mind when he prays, and what his intention is in educating others to pray. Why, in fact, is he teaching them this?

That is to say: anybody who goes beyond the mere task of imparting purely formal and external information about prayer encounters the question of the nature and task of prayer long before he deals with other questions in this area. To be sure, the question is not always asked in as direct and unequivocal a manner. But this question is always there and appears in one form or another. If I would attempt to describe what is being done now, in practice, in the area of education for prayer, I would say that it is confined to two objects. One object of education in this area is to see to it that the pupils are "good children," that is, that they pray three times a day. There are teachers and parents for whom the primary meaning of education for prayer—and, in practice, the only thing they do in this area—is to make their children or students accustomed to pray regularly, in an almost mechanical fashion. In most of the religious institutions in Israel, whether those of the *Hinukh Atzmai* (Independent) system or of the state religious school network, education for prayer is concentrated on the acquisition of the habit of organized prayer, every morning. (Through this, various oddities come about. For example, an acquaintance of mine, who had been raised in a religious home, told me that it was only by accident that he discovered one day the existence of the *Minhah* [Afternoon] prayer, as he had not heard about this in school, or at home, because he never saw people reciting this prayer. But this is really part of another problem, that of the real religious character of the so-called *dati* home.)

The school thus sees itself as responsible for inculcating the habit of regular, mechanical prayer. To a considerable extent, it succeeds in this. The student acquires the technical ability, the knowledge of how it is done, as well as the moral stamina required to enable him to rise every morning and pray, without skipping a day. This is an accomplishment to be duly valued, and I do not mean to belittle it. I remember that once a quite mature young man, who had grown up on a *kibbutz* and had studied at Bar-Ilan University for a number of years, came to our synagogue to learn how to pray. One of the things that astonished him was how the small children in the synagogue knew what to do. He asked again and again how they knew when to stand, when to sit, what page to open to, and so on. All of this is part of education, and it has achieved a certain success. It is one of the objects of education for prayer.

The other aspect of education for prayer concerns itself, and I would almost say concludes, with what is called in several places "the *kavanah* (intention) of prayer." And here the main object has been to understand what is written in the prayer book. Of course, I do not oppose the idea that people should know and understand what is written in the *siddur*; on the contrary, I personally tried, at one time, to exert pressure that the *siddur* be introduced into the religious schools as a compulsory subject of study, so that those children who use it should know what they are saying. One of the inspectors of the religious schools told me that this was unnecessary because "they all know," but I contend that this is simply not so. This subject, however important though it is, is not what I have in mind in this essay.

From the point of view of comprehension, education for prayer may be accomplished by a good school, a good teacher, and sometimes by a good father or even a good rabbi, who can explain to the children what prayers to say, how they are connected with one another, why each blessing is formulated in its particular way, what are its subject and context, and so forth. One teacher will explain things in terms of numerology (*gematria*) and mysteries, another by means of history—each according to the style he prefers. However, with all the importance and value this has, this is not true and deep education for prayer. Such explanations are useful as an aid, but this is not education for prayer as such, education that comes to grips with the nature and foundation of prayer. I would like to give a personal illustration of this.

After some years of separation, I met an old friend who is now the dean of one of the *yeshivot* in Israel. I asked him what he does during his prayers, whether he concentrates on prayer itself. Yes, he answered, he has *kavanah* (devotion). I asked him, "What *kavanah* do you have?" He explained that his intent during prayer was to understand the connection between one sentence and the next, between one word and another, between the various sections, and so on. He thinks about and concentrates on these matters—and this he calls *kavanah* in prayer. I told him, rather shortly, that these are things I do on *Shabbat* after eating dinner, and that sometimes I study these problems and look into books that deal with and explain prayer in this manner. But to regard the analysis of the text (which is what his *kavanah* amounted to, though he did not use this expression) as a proper form of devotion for, say, the service of the High Holy Days—this I cannot agree with or accept as *kavanah* in the true sense.

In order to explain something about this subject of *kavanah*, I will quote a well-known anecdote: They tell of a

simple Jew, almost an ignoramus, who sto
Hashanah and recited with great fervor the liturgical po
"These and these shout with a shouting, these and these roar with a roaring. . . ." They asked him why this great fervor over "*befetzah mefatshim*," and what did he understand of these prayers? The Jew answered, "What do I care what is written there? I know that all of the prayers have one meaning: Master of the Universe, help us to make a living."

To my mind, in terms of what is truly connected to the nature of prayer, the Jew in this story was far closer to the depths of prayer than the one who knows the exact date of composition of the prayers and knows all about two- and three-letter roots in ancient and modern *piyutim*.

When I wish to teach that which is called "the standing in prayer," it seems to me that the questions raised are not first and foremost technical. The basic thing is not the understanding of the prayers, what words I use and how I understand them. Long before this, prayer raises two fundamental questions, one greater and more fundamental, the other perhaps a partial question within a larger one. When a man prays, he says in every prayer and in every *nusah* of prayer: "Blessed art Thou, O Lord." When a man says, "Blessed art Thou, O Lord," he finds himself standing before God—in direct confrontation with Him. That is to say, the moment a person says these words and does not wish to be a liar or a deceiver or the like, he makes an affirmation and places himself before God—and this fact far outweighs any textual or technical consideration, such as whether this form of prayer is attractive or not. In every prayer, before all else, we face this great issue. It amounts to this: When a man prays, he addresses the Holy One, blessed be He.

I was confronted with this question, not as a teacher

but as a parent. Once, while I was in the middle of my prayers, my little daughter tried to talk to me, and when I failed to respond, she was very angry with me: "Why don't you speak to me?" Later on, I answered her by saying: "I was busy. I was speaking with God." She then replied, with great understanding, that she hadn't noticed that God was answering me. This second question was very deep and it goes beyond the limits of our discussion here. In any event, a four- or five-year-old girl was prepared to accept the notion that I speak with God when I pray, but she wanted this to be a two-way conversation and not just a speech on my part.

The point is that every prayer boils down in the final analysis to a very basic point: the words "Blessed art Thou," and especially the "Thou," that is, if I feel the presence of the "Thou" before me. If I have someone with whom to speak, then I can pray; if I have no one with whom to speak, then what is the point of all these words, and all the things I say, new, old, good, bad, ugly? What good is all this if I have no feeling of presence, in the simplest sense?

What I am saying here is so simple that it should not need to be said, except that it still does need to be said, and stressed: prayer is an expression of faith. It is impossible to pray, except out of faith in the encounter with God, in the standing of the I opposite the Thou. I don't want to enter into the niceties of this subject; it is not a question of Buberian philosophy; it is a simple point, so simple that any child can understand it, And yet, it is a problem that confronts adults, the more they wish to delve into the problem of prayer, the intention of prayer and especially the question of education for prayer. It is a theological problem, perhaps the most important problem of all, and it arises in regard to every single prayer and blessing we say. Whoever deals with people trying to find their way to religious faith knows that these are critical, existential questions.

When I pray, I speak with someone. I must necessarily believe in His existence, and not only in His existence. Moreover, I do not thereby accept just an abstract metaphysical existence, in the fashion of those who opt for orthopraxis (which is so intellectually easy). It is not enough that I place God in some corner, from which He won't touch me or come to me, and that I take care that I have no contact with Him except in that peculiar region known as "the observance of the *mitzvot*"—something no one quite understands. For, when a man prays, he explicitly places himself before somebody. And he must assume that this "somebody" hears what he says to Him.

Thus, education for prayer raises the whole question of the reality of the awareness of God in the heart and mind of the person praying, and his ability to pass on this awareness to others. This is the first, more inclusive question regarding prayer. There is also a less general, more personal question. In almost every prayer, besides the doxologies and affirmations (as in a portion of the eighteen benedictions), there are also petitionary prayers. I pray, in short, means: I request. And this includes all of the middle twelve of the eighteen benedictions.

One ought to remember that every request contains within it the expectations of a miracle and the assumption that a miracle can, in fact, occur. When a man requests, "Master of the Universe, heal the sick of your people Israel," he requests something specific. That is, he asks that something happen, a certain change in the world, be it large or small. But, in essence, it is a request that something occur, and that something occur that would not have occurred had he not prayed. True, I am putting this in the simplest manner, in the form that is understood and felt even by the smallest children, but it is also the case for adults who would put it in more sophisticated, precise, and elegant form. There is no other way to understand all of the blessings and prayers, except as a request for a transnatural occurrence, within nature or above nature, but always involving a certain departure from ordinary laws. That is to say, before one enters into discussion of the details of the external components of prayer, whether large or small, one must remember that prayer is not like any other act, or speech said before somebody, and therefore education for prayer is not simply education for a certain defined area of action or a specific *mitzvah*. Education for prayer is of necessity far broader: it is a necessary and essential part of a far more general way of education, of educational striving for faith.

If we wish to educate for prayer, we need to pass on the basic assumptions that exist in every prayer in the world. Whoever accepts these basic principles can and ought to pass them on in the process of education, and if he is unable to do this, then there is no point in his getting involved in the details that follow. Whoever gives up these basic points has given up on any meaningful contact with prayer.

In his day, R. Yitzhak Meir of Gur said similar things, in the following way: When the Evil One succeeds in stealing the essentials from a man, he leaves him with all of the foolishness—even to say "*Hodu*" before "*Barukh She'amar*" in the morning service—because then all of these things don't matter. The foolish things can remain. From then on, a person can say the prayers with or without the passage dealing with the Temple sacrifices because they have become irrelevant. He relates to prayer as in the saying, "He swears with his lips, but denies it in his heart." It is as if he had said in his heart, before he starts praying, that whatever he is about to say is a heap of lies and falsehood, from beginning to end, for it would seem that he speaks and there is no one to hear, no one to answer, so that his whole prayer is a matter of empty words, addressed to the emptiness. To be sure, I have put the matter crudely, but without doubt there are many people (belonging to what are called "religious circles") for whom this is their inner sense of prayer. Prayer, for them, is a certain duty that every man is required to perform, like all the other not-understood and meaningless performances. He is obliged to put on a *tallit*, and he is obliged to say such and such words. From this standpoint, the education toward mechanical recitation of prayers solves the problem. The interpretations given of "what is my duty that I shall do it" show very well how to deal with this situation as well. In the same way as they teach one how to wrap oneself up in a *tallit*, they can teach when to accent the penultimate syllable and when the last, and in this manner the problem is solved.

However, if prayer has any sort of content, and a man relates to this content, the meaning of this is that every prayer is an inner declaration on certain points of faith.

The problematic nature of education for prayer is part of a general crisis, and the crisis in prayer is that part of the crisis of faith we can all see. The existing problems with regard to the *nusah* of prayer, and so on, are generally speaking expressions of a more general theological crisis. They do not stem from the fact that this or another prayer is not up-to-date. Prayer, in general, expresses a certain posture and a certain path, and in general it is not so particularized that one cannot reconcile it with changed circumstances and details. But prayer, without doubt, postulates certain broad theological attitudes and bases itself upon them. I see no place for prayer without prior theological affirmations. I know that there is, these days, a general withdrawal from all theology and from metaphysical definitions. There is an attempt to compromise and not to take risks or raise inner doubts and difficulties, to resolve the lack of faith by relating to a text that one tries to void of all inner content.

In order to demonstrate—against a slightly different background—just how far this goes, I may mention an article that appeared recently in the monthly journal *Masa*, describing a piece of biblical research that was done in all seriousness. This was an attempt to demonstrate that all *malakhim* (angels, messengers) mentioned in the Bible were in fact human beings, the basic assumption being: How is it possible that a book as sublime as the Bible could deal with the supernatural? This was an extremely serious article, which attempted to resolve speculative theological problems (which also exist for many who pray). Of course, the solution was only partial, because God did not enter into the picture. As a matter of fact, left-wing Zionist movement Hashomer Hatzair once published a *tanakh* (Bible) that corrected this error also. This edition eliminated every mention of the name of God, and thus resolved the problem. This Bible (which was published and then withdrawn from circulation) was an attempt to solve a theological problem by eliminating it completely. This is an approach one can use toward the *siddur* as well, and it could be done by a staff of serious religious scholars. It would be possible to create a popular *siddur* that would speak to the heart and create no problems. To begin with, one would remove all those passages dealing with animal sacrifices (as some people have done) and the passages dealing with a bodily resurrection of the dead and a personal Messiah (as has been done in various places), and in the end one would also remove the name of the Holy One, blessed be He, from the *siddur*, and then we should have a truly magnificent prayer book. So that this not seem to you like a mere fantasy, I suggest that you examine almost any Passover *Haggadah* from the *kibbutzim* of forty years ago. It is possible to see there that such a thing is not only possible, but was in fact done, and with total seriousness. It is possible to perform a Passover *seder* and to pronounce blessings in which there is not only no mention of the Passover Sacrifice, but no mention of the Name of Heaven, in the same way as was done (and perhaps still is done) in the "ceremony of bringing of the first-fruits" on the Feast of Weeks, where the theological content has been removed from the ceremony, so as to make it speak equally to all. In brief: enlightened, aesthetic, and clear.

All of these examples are mentioned simply to explain that the concern with external details is not only superficial but also misleading. The question of old and out-of-date forms of prayer is, in the final analysis, an extremely peripheral issue. The basic cause of the discomfort people feel with the *siddur* is—as I have explained earlier—the very deep problem people have with regard to faith and theology, and every attempt to hide behind problems of text or of varying *minhag* shows lack of seriousness. This basic point, that prayer is an expression of a living faith, is known to everyone and is almost tautological. With all this, these problems are not openly expressed or stated. Perhaps a group of scholars and thinkers can allow itself to hide from such a central problem, in the course of a series of abstract discussions, but an educator—on any level—cannot allow himself to do this. The educator, even if he is not aware of it, senses that education for prayer is one of the important—and essential—elements of education toward faith. And education for faith, through the means of prayer, means education toward a certain *kind* of faith, since the prayer has a specific content.

One of the specific components of this faith is the personal relation between the one who hears and the one who speaks. I must believe (and be prepared to pass on this belief to others) that when I stand with my face toward the wall, I am *not* speaking to the wall, but I *am* speaking to God, and He hears my prayer and answers it in some fashion. This is part of the education for faith and there must be an injection of this understanding into ordinary life.

If a man wishes to relate to God, he cannot jail Him in the synagogue, without any connection with the surrounding world. If I wish to explain to a small child or to a grown man what prayer is, I must of necessity say that there is One "who hears prayer," and by this relate not only to the specific blessing in the *Amidah* ("Blessed is He who hears our prayer") but to the actual concept itself. And if there is one who hears prayer, then the blessing "He who hears prayer" is part of the nature of life—not only when I pray, but at other times as well.

If a man cannot live with this awareness, then this touches upon theological problems, on the problem of his general worldview, which is not a matter only of prayer. He who takes the view that he cannot tell a child, a student, a man who comes to pour out his heart, that God in fact exists and really is, has a personal problem that he has to settle with himself first. Instead of educating another person in prayer, he had better first stand and pray that he be granted the ability to pray. Doubtless, there exist such prayers, both ancient and very modern, both in circles far from and close to Judaism. There are prayers in which people pray for faith, for the ability to pray. It is possible that such a prayer creates its own problems, but it is at least a real prayer, and it is needed as a preliminary to any discussion on this subject.

In every attempt at meeting, whether with adults or with children, there is no other solution to the problem of education for prayer (and even to the question of education for *mitzvot*, with all the difference between the two) than to come to a confrontation—self-confrontation, if you like—and this must be faced up to both before the educational act and during it.

To summarize: to the extent that it is possible to educate to pray, this may only be done within a more general framework of education toward faith. Those schools called religious, in the course of their lessons, which include every subject under the sun, do not deal properly with this topic, neither openly nor, generally, in an indirect way either. It is astonishing that the professedly religious school does not deal directly with the question of faith. Why must the religious child, like every other child, pass his own crises of faith in such awful loneliness, with no one to ask—neither teacher nor rabbi—with not even the background to enable him to frame the question?

It is possible that because of the inability to decide whether to follow *Nusah Sefarad* or *Nusah Ashkenaz*, whether to decide the principles in this *nusah* or another, people have decided not to teach anything and not to try to attain to anything basic. The same is customary in the subject known as "Jewish Thought," which is mainly taught by placing before the student scores of passages from all sorts of sources and to say, "This is how Jews thought," without attempting to bring the students to any basic consideration of what *they* think or should think as Jews, and without setting any line or standard as to actual thought or faith. Again, prayer can only be taught as part of an education toward faith in general. Education means taking a stand; it means that the educator is prepared to defend his religious position. If he believes in it, well and good; if he does not believe, then he must face the question of whether he ought to pretend that he is more God-fearing than he really is. This is a large question, which comes up wherever a teacher (even the *melamed* in the most old-fashioned *heder*) attempts to talk about prayer. Every teacher must attempt then to settle this problem with his own conscience, and the solution is not easy.

In any event, when a worldview founded on faith exists, there is a possibility of building on it a relationship to prayer. Only when such faith exists is there reason to pray, that is, to pronounce certain words seriously. And if not, then one is reciting parrot-fashion, and it is a pity for the energy spent in mechanically teaching things that have no meaning to those who say them. He who prays (i.e., "speaks with God") necessarily requests various things. If he is serious, then his requests are sincere. But one who recites the blessings from "*Tzemah David*" (for the restoration of the Davidic dynasty) to "*Retzeh*" (for the restoration of sacrifices)—and very much hopes that these things will *not* happen—has no educational problems at all, since he contradicts the very essence of education. On the other hand, the one who is praying seriously may have problems, may suffer confrontation; but this confrontation will be one of faith, not a confrontation with prayer. Prayer is a superstructure that stands above the overall structure of faith, and it is by no means a subject in itself. It is impossible to separate it from the problem of faith generally, and it has no existence without that.

To be sure, it is possible to discuss Jewish prayer with detachment, as one would discuss Tibetan prayer when a man is concerned with comparative religion. But when one deals with prayer as a subject in life, and as a subject of education, one must relate to the subject in a personal fashion. And a personal approach requires faith. I know that to speak about faith to a group of people involved in Jewish thought is somewhat embarrassing—it is a subject that is almost taboo, one that people are ashamed to talk about in public. With all this, I think that there are more believers than those who make themselves out to be such in public. That is, even in the religious community there are more people who believe than one thinks.

My late uncle once quoted the great Rabbi of Kotsk, who said—in light of the story of Judah and Tamar—that every man must have a close friend, so close that he can reveal his heart to him and even tell him that he has had dealings with a prostitute! And my uncle added that this was said in those days. Today, one can talk about such things in the street with anybody. But today one needs a close soul-friend, to whom one can tell that one believes in God, to tell him that, despite the fact of being religious and carrying out the *mitzvot*, "I nevertheless believe in God!" I think that part of the job of religious education is in the personal ability to throw off the philosophical, intellectual, and academic baggage that has become an encumbrance rather than a staff to support us, and to say what many people think in their hearts—that God really does exist (in spite of the declarations that He exists) and that it is actually possible to turn to Him. Only in this way is it possible to speak of prayer and to educate for prayer.

V

11

The Five *Megillot*: An Introduction

The five *megillot* are five books of the Bible that, for a variety of reasons, are considered a single entity. Nevertheless, these *megillot* are very different from each other; each one is a world in itself and far from the others, not only historically, in time, but also in terms of style and content. Thus the story of the *Megillah* of Ruth takes place in the time of the Judges when Israel was just settling in the land; the *Megillah* of the Song of Songs and that of Ecclesiastes, both attributed to King Solomon, belong to the height of the splendor of the First Kingdom. The Book of Lamentations was composed hundreds of years later, at the very end of the First Kingdom, while the events of the *Megillah* of Esther take place far away at the time of the beginning of the Second Temple period.

In their very essence, the *megillot* are even more varied. The two story *megillot*, Ruth and Esther, are not only historically separated, but their form and content are very different. To be sure, they both have a woman heroine, but how great the contrast! The story of Ruth is in a pastoral setting, and contained within the life of a family, whereas the *Megillah* of Esther unrolls the drama of a magnificent court of a great empire and the events therein are cosmopolitan, of the agony of war and defeat, of suffering unto death, and of life in disgrace. The Song of Songs may be designated a private song in which the whole world is only a setting for the pair of lovers, while the *Megillah* of Lamentations has national-historical importance. The *Megillah* of Ruth is, after all, no more than an idyll of country life in the hills of Judea, full of warm descriptions of village customs, of human charity and grace, whereas the *Megillah* of Esther is an epic account of palaces and kings, of grandeur and corruption, intrigue and betrayal. Ruth, who comes from a secure and stable world and, according to a certain tradition, from a royal family, chooses to participate in a life of poverty and obscurity; Esther comes from a modest home to participate in the palace grandeur of a great empire. The humble background of Ruth is the beginning of a glorious line of kings; the splendor of Esther's life at court has no continuation, except in the memory of a people. At the same time, there is a certain common factor, not easily discerned at first, between the two heroines. In spite of the differences in their subsequent destinies, the two women leave their homeland and their parental homes and give their lives for a greater ideal.

The two poetic *megillot*—the Song of Songs and Lamentations—are also markedly different. The Song of Songs is a poem that is wholly about love, and it is consistently optimistic in tone, in spite of the occasional (sweet) pain of distress at parting, because of the imminent fulfillment of this love. The Book of Lamentations, however, is a poem of pain, full of the agony of war and defeat, of suffering unto death, and of life in disgrace. The Song of Songs may be designated a private song in which the whole world is only a setting for a pair of lovers, while the *Megillah* of Lamentations is clearly the lament of the entire nation, in which the disaster of the individual is only a personal example of the national catastrophe. To be sure, at a deeper level, these two poems, as well, have a certain common factor. The Song of Songs is also a love song between the people of Israel and the God of Israel, and the *Megillah* of Lamentations is another aspect to the relations between this pair.

Furthermore, even within the bitterness of the lamentations there is no hint of a desire to nullify this bond or to cause any permanent rupture. The love, in spite of everything, remains intact. Even so, the partings and disappearances of the lover in the Song of Songs may be seen as a subtle indication of the terribleness of the Lord's hiding of His face in the Book of Lamentations. In a wider compass, in the *Megillah* of Lamentations, there are also signs of hope and faith in the fact that this is only a temporary concealment of the Divine and that love will ultimately triumph.

The *Megillah* of Ecclesiastes and that of the Song of Songs are both attributed to King Solomon, as said, but how vast the difference between them. The Song of Songs is set in an eternal springtime of youth and hope. In Ecclesiastes there is a feeling of old age and death, a dismal reckoning of a life bereft of purpose. The world of the Song of Songs is fairly straightforward, and in spite of the dance movements to and fro, life proceeds to a certain wholesome resolution, while Ecclesiastes expresses with bitter irony a world of paradox and meaninglessness in which victory and defeat are equally pointless and without value. The sages of Israel have been divided in their opinion about the time in King Solomon's life when each was composed. Some say that the Song of Songs was written when Solomon was still young, and Ecclesiastes when he was old. Others maintain the opposite, that it was in his youth that Solomon wrote Ecclesiastes, not as an autobiographical work but as the viewpoint of a young man whose critical sense outweighed his powers of forgiveness, whereas the Song of Songs is a poem of reconciliation with life, a product of the tranquillity that comes after the pain and ordeal of experience, when a person has the composure to create such a poem on all the planes of its meaning.

The many-sided variety of these five *megillot* and the complexity of their hidden and esoteric contents have given the books a special place in Jewish life. According to strict *Halakhah,* there is only a *mitzvah* to read the *Megillah* of Esther publicly on Purim and to recite Lamentations on Tisha B'Av. Nevertheless, very many congregations have adopted the wide custom of reading the *Megillah* of Song of Songs on the Sabbath of Passover, the *Megillah* of Ruth on Shavuot, and the *Megillah* of Ecclesiastes on the Sabbath of Sukkot.

12

Ruth: The Hidden Spring

Ruth is one of the two women in the Bible for whom a whole book is named. She is also the one woman in the Scriptures who has no human fault ascribed to her: she stands alone not only among the heroines of the Bible, but among most of the men. Although Ruth's early life was neither easy nor simple, nor even very satisfactory, its defects were foisted upon her from without; she maintained her wholeness and purity of being.

We have no real information regarding Ruth's origins. The tradition of the sages is that she was a princess, a daughter of Eglon, king of Moab. Be that as it may, in the biblical story, Ruth is not seen as being rooted in her own nation or as being essentially part of her own people. She appears much more as an exception, as an outsider to her beginnings and origins. Thus, she has become the archetype of the convert, reinforcing the view that converts do not really undergo any substantial process of change, of passing from one essential state to another. They do not undergo a process of renewal or renewed creativity but are people who have belonged to another world without knowing it. Like Ruth, they are people who find themselves.

In a larger context, the story of Ruth is an example of a process, a vast ordering of forces and events, that extends throughout the Bible. It is a story in which people finally find their rightful place, and in which personal, family, and historical connections finally come to fulfillment. It is not always clear how this happens; but in one way or another, many cycles are completed here.

The sages commented that Ruth perfected, or, in other words, redeemed, several figures from the distant past. Hence, her association with the kings of Moab; in the language of the Lurianic Kabbalah, she redeemed the holy spark of Moab. Here an ancient, forgotten link is once again revealed, and the concealed essence of Moab is made manifest.

According to the Book of Genesis, Moab was the son of Lot, the close relative of Abraham, not only his brother's son but perhaps also his brother-in-law. In a sense, Lot serves as Abraham's counterpart, his companion who endeavored to imitate him. The similarity between Abraham and Lot is, of course, only partial, because Lot had many failings, and ended his life in a way that was both sad and unpleasant, his heirs children born of an incestuous relationship. Nevertheless, it is possible here to trace a continuous line.

In another biblical story—the selling of Joseph—the same idea appears. In the *Midrash*, it is considered that, in this story, the different patterns of history with their many-sided events and actions, good and bad, finally gather into the "light of the Messiah"—that is, out of the intentional and the unintentional, the beautiful and the ugly, something positive emerges. The good deeds remain, and the faulty elements tend to disappear, allowing other aspects to come to the fore. Even where something is primarily evil, no particle or spark of goodness is lost. The sparks, connecting, finally manifest themselves, sometimes after many generations, and in a striking way. Similarly, a recessive gene may pass from one generation to the next without any sign of its existence until, with the passage of time and genetic recombining, it is revealed as inherent strength. If it is a question of a rare quality or attribute in a human being, such a child justifies the long chain of history.

So it was with Lot, who had superior attributes that were not destroyed. Lot was devoted to the principles of hospitality. His daughters, despite the vileness of their deed, acted as much from the wish to preserve the human species—as it seemed to them—as from passion or lust. It is even possible to detect a veiled similarity between the act of Lot's daughters and Ruth's approach to Boaz many generations later. There was a deep commitment to the continuation of the line, the need to hold fast to the thread of generations, both in the delicacy of Ruth's hint and in the crudeness of Lot's daughters' act. Yet, it was the good intention that persisted through time.

Ruth, the daughter of Eglon, king of Moab, was a descendant of the line of Balak, who, according to the sages, evinced reverence for the God of Israel and for prophecy. Eglon, too, rose in honor of the one who brought him God's word. The assumption was that noble characteristics and qualities never disappear or are altogether lost but are merely hidden from sight. At the right moment, in the right place, they burst forth like a spring, purified of evil.

The aspect of finding oneself liberated from all external bondage to the past and of emerging unhesitant and without inhibition is very evident in Ruth. It is forcefully revealed in her conversation with Naomi, her dead husband's mother, when Naomi tells her two daughters-in-law to leave. Naomi's position here was clear and practical, even from a halakhic point of view: these daughters-in-law were no longer bound to her legally or financially, and nothing remained but for them to return to where they belonged. Orpah, the other daughter-in-law, did return to her home and once more became part of the gentile world. (The sages trace the origins of Goliath and his brothers back to Orpah, as the antithesis of David, who was one of Ruth's descendants. Orpah represents the Gentiles' contact with Israel—a contact that became increasingly estranged, until the final confrontation, which the sages call the "succumbing of the sons who kiss to the sons of those who cleave.")

What is surprising in Ruth is not only her cleaving to her mother-in-law but the fact that she joined her whole inner life to Naomi's, to the life of a woman of another nation, with different beliefs and customs. Furthermore, it was a life that held no promise for the foreseeable future. Nonetheless, Ruth persisted in accompanying Naomi to the end; and although the end was, in a sense, happy, not only for Ruth personally but also for the magnificent chain of generations that followed, this end was not apparent at the beginning. The act that began the chain was free and willing and did not anticipate any recompense.

It is impossible to assume that, in those days, a woman would marry a man of another nation and not convert to his religion, customs, and values; it seems certain that Ruth underwent some kind of conversion to Judaism at the time of her marriage, even though the Jewish family in question was, to some extent, cut off from its roots. This was a family that had found it appropriate and fitting to leave Bethlehem and move to another country, which, albeit not totally strange and hostile, was not Jewish. This was no mere departure from the homeland in a physical sense, but meant leaving also its values and its Jewish way of life. The meaning of such emigration is strikingly revealed in the words of David, a child of Ruth's son, when he was forced to flee from *Eretz Yisroel*: "They have driven me out this day from abiding in the inheritance of the Lord, saying, Go, serve other gods" (1 Samuel 26:19). The assumption was that leaving the homeland meant, as the Talmud later expressed it, "refined idolatry."

At the same time, this family of *yordim*, or émigrés, would have maintained a heritage of memories, remnants of Jewish traditions. Their spiritual world, while certainly less perfect and complete than it had been in Judah, their homeland, was still a world that held great significance for Ruth. It was a world that had for her enough spiritual content to make her go with her mother-in-law to her people, and for Ruth to feel that she had found her place among them even before she knew that she would have a family of her own there. Ruth's statement, "Thy people shall be my people, and thy God my God" (Ruth 1:16), is not merely an expression of personal harmony with another people, but reveals a deep and genuine spiritual connection.

The bond between Ruth and Naomi, too, was not only personal, but deep and intimate. For generations, the relationship between a woman and her daughter-in-law had been one of subordination and duty (of the latter to the former), and the prophets speak of the rebellion of a bride against her mother-in-law as an indication of the decline of the times. Even so, any close connection, much less love, between them was very unusual. In fact, the *Mishnah* lists women who are, in the nature of things, antagonistic to one another, and among them a mother- and daughter-in-law.

In any case, it is clear that Ruth's feelings toward the land of Judah, its people, and its religion, transcended the ties of family and personal relations. Boaz expressed it when he praised Ruth, saying that she deserved recompense and reward because she had come to shelter under the wings of the Lord (Ruth 2:12), that is, it was evident that Ruth's coming to Bethlehem was a step of fundamental significance. There is no external explanation for her coming; it was simply done out of a feeling of involvement by a person who had found her proper place among the people of Israel. Above and beyond the chance family connection—canceled out in any case by the death of Elimelech, who left Ruth childless—this feeling of belonging caused her to follow Naomi to Bethlehem and to find her final fulfillment in the house of Boaz. Naomi returned home from Moab; and it seems that Ruth, too, was coming home, coming to seek refuge under the protection of the Almighty.

To some extent, the relationship of Ruth and Boaz stands on the fact that he saw in her, from their very first meeting, things that other people did not see. For others, Ruth was first and foremost a foreigner and, as such, an object of suspicion, if not hatred. Most felt that it was better to keep a safe distance from this foreigner, who was only a poor convert in an alien land, without family and protection. In stating that he did not wish to mar his own inheritance, the kinsman who was called upon to enter some kind of levirate marriage with Ruth meant that he did not want to marry a woman who was defective in the sense that she was a convert, a Moabitess, a foreigner, or to contaminate himself with something so doubtful. This suspicion and hostility were very real. However, according to the sages, Boaz was one of the respected men of Bethlehem, a judge of the tribe of Judah; and he saw things in a different way. Beyond the fact that she was a poor, foreign convert, he saw Ruth's inner being, and this is what he cared about. To Boaz, Ruth had come to seek protection under the wings of the *Shekhinah*; and even before he could consider any personal relationship with her, he tried to encourage her, to support her, and to bring her closer to his world.

Boaz and the kinsman express two different attitudes to proselytes: on the one hand, rejection and suspicion; on the other, a deep feeling of sympathy and attraction. This relationship is subtly portrayed in the Book of Ruth. In the *Midrash*, it is expressed in a parable: A shepherd has a large flock of sheep. A deer enters the fold. The shepherd tells his herdsmen to treat the deer with special care. The herdsmen ask why, with such a large flock, the shepherd should concern himself with this one deer. The shepherd tells them, "My sheep have only this fold, while this deer has the whole world to choose from. Yet he chose my flock, and it is therefore fitting that I should give him special care."

This attitude sums up the many *mitzvot* that require us to welcome the proselyte into our midst, someone who has the choice of belonging elsewhere and who, nevertheless, chooses to enter the Jewish framework. The convert deserves special consideration and a special relationship. The Book of Ruth is a beautiful portrayal of a true proselyte, unique in the Scriptures in that she is described as being wholly pure.

The description of Ruth's homecoming to her real, inner being is a spiritual odyssey: we see her shed the trappings of her former existence, the connection with her family and origins. We see her undeterred by the difficulties of her new life; we see her fidelity to her commitment even when she is faced with the indifference of the local people. Finally, we see all these pale into insignificance in relation to Ruth's inner soul. We see that same ancient kernel of sanctity, that same spark that had burned unseen for generations, find its rightful place within the people of Israel.

13

The Song of Songs

The word *shir* (song) has two meanings in the holy tongue. Besides the aesthetic-literary meaning, the word carries the significance of a ring or bracelet, or a chain of such bands. The title phrase "Song of Songs" could therefore connote a series of songs within a single song, like a string of beads. The song sequel in the biblical Song of Solomon would then be more than a collection of poetic verses relating to a variety of different events; in essence that is the song itself. Which is to say, the song is a double, triple, or quadruple song, in which the different segments of the sequence are not next to one another but each within the others. The very same song constitutes a whole string of songs with worlds upon worlds of meaning connected and intertwining with each other and passing from world to world, from one domain of reality to another, separate and different.

The Song of Songs is at one and the same time a private song and a general one; it is both carnal and spiritual. On one hand it is certainly a love song between a man and a woman, lovers who admire one another greatly, who lose and find each other. On the other hand, it is also a song of love in the wider sense, of the connection between Israel and her God; it is a song of love and devotion, of redemption and exile, of human error and repentance. And still another song may be found therein, and this too very personal, but definitely spiritual, concerning the relationship between the soul and the Divine, a song of yearning and neglect, of search and supplication. A fourth song is there too, which is a more general song about the rapport between the Creator and His creation, between the *Ein Sof* (Infinite) and the *Shekhinah* (the Divine Indwelling); it sings of the way the world comes and goes, disappears and gets hidden, only to return and merge with the Creator.

Clearly then, the song series concerns itself with different layers of reality, each of which belongs to an entirely separate world. And yet the spiritual and broadly comprehensive songs are not abstract or allegorical developments of the simple love song at the beginning. They are complete in themselves. Even though they are integrated one within the other, each is somehow true to itself and self-contained within its own framework. Moreover, all of the songs draw sustenance from each other. Every one is somehow a sign or an explication for another, and at the same time the breath of life for another. Even more, each one of the songs gets its clarity and its wholeness from the next song. Without the others, which belong to an entirely separate world, none of them could stand.

The human love story between man and woman became a song only because of the other, sublime poetry behind it. Were it not for the heavenly love the earthly love would have expressed only a cry of biological craving. What raises the physical yearning is the loftier craving for which the human physical love serves as an allegory. Even when the lovers are not aware of it, their love includes in it something more, elements that they cannot define to themselves. The biology of desire is very direct, very simple—and in and of itself, quite uninteresting. But here, because there is something beyond it, the love cry exceeds its purpose as an instrument for the satisfaction of physical desire—it becomes a song-poem. And in a wider scope, since the love between the lover and his beloved is really a material symbol of the entire love of a people and, more than that, of the entire world, the song is lifted up, gains dimensions of another greatness and scope in which matter ceases to be only physical, and becomes the material bearer of other essences.

And just as the sensual poem is raised up by its being bound to the more spiritual songs, so too is the spiritual poem elevated and enhanced by virtue of the sensual poem. The spiritual songs of themselves would probably have assumed more abstract and ephemeral forms. But this spirituality is not necessarily an advantage: a spiritual expression is perhaps more refined and delicate but it is also pale and insubstantial and cold. It is the sensual poem that gives the spiritual poetry its passion and vigor, involves it with the material world, with all its forms and colors. The evenly proportioned design of the spiritual world is enriched by its contact with this other world of blind, chaotic matter.

The Jewish people as a whole can only function and even think in very general terms. The parts constituting this whole, because of their multiplicity and the differences between them, relinquish and obscure the subtleties of their individual differences, and their functioning as a single unit is necessarily simpler, made up of a limited number of actions and operations of a general significance, whereas the individual love song adds to the general song of the people not only the colorfulness of the individual personality, but, in addition, the dimension of authentic feeling and intimate experience.

The story—on all its levels—is not a chronologically ordered tale of events that follow one another in narrative or ballad form. But that which seems to be disorderly in the story is also the source of its great power, changing it from a simple love story to a comprehensive psalm of praise, a psalm that does not only relate to one individual person or to any specific historic event or to a well-defined typical structure, but acts as a general song that belongs to every happening, every person, every combination of reality. In the order of any one life, or in any particular chapter of a national history, the poem could be read as it is, while in other situations, various sections are appropriate. And there is no end to the story—because the things described therein never come to any conclusion. Even if in a single human life the story plot of love does come to some end, for others it goes on. Every person begins this same tale again at some point in his biography, and lives it in the life of his spirit. Similarly, every period in the history of the nation begins the story anew, from another starting point, and every era in the development of the world recommences it again and not always from the same point of departure. And only when all is finished and fulfilled, only at the last, will the conclusion of this tale finally unfold. Only then will the story came to an end.

Just as it has no ending, the story plot of the Song of Songs has no beginning. But it is not like most of the books of the Bible, which do not start from the beginning of the narrative, but long after; this particular book simply does not have a beginning. And this is because generally every love story, whether it be earthly or heavenly, has some kind of commencement with a description of the first meeting, even if it is a love-at-first-sight situation, and a certain development of the plot with all its uncertainties and problematics until the mutual disclosure of love and its fatefulness for the lovers. This course of true love is not only characteristic of the human-earthly form; it is no less so for the other levels of love in the Song of Songs. The people of Israel and God, the soul and the Creator, these "lovers" also have a first meeting of some sort, and a series of hesitant encounter until the decisive commitment. The absence of such a vital part of the account in the Song of Songs may seem to belittle this prime element of doubt and indecision, of the tension inherent in the mutual search. To be sure, the narrative poem does have tension in it with a certain amount of losing and finding each other, but the first part of the relation, which is so important in any mutual cherishing, is somehow missing.

This deletion is not accidental; it may even be one of the keys to the essence of the poem. In all the seeking and fumbling mentioned in the Song, in the partings and coming together of the protagonists, all the questioning and wondering, there is one thing that is certain—the deep connection between the lover and the beloved on all the levels of the account. There is never any doubt that the two are destined for one another and bound to each other. Throughout the winding threads of their fortunes, their partings and reunions, we are never left uncertain about the indissoluble bond between them.

The fact that the Song of Songs has neither beginning nor end signifies that the story does not belong to any particular time; basically it is not a tale of anything that happened in the past or that will happen in the future. It takes place in an eternal present, which is always real and concurrent. True, a certain part of the narrative has already taken place (like in the more general national layer of the poem, the Exodus from Egypt), but not only is this past still fresh in memory, it is actually always there, in the historical present or in the future. That is to say, the order of things may change a little from time to time, but the song remains fixed in an ever repeated and forever existent pattern of events.

This eternal present of the Song of Songs occurs in a certain season of the year, the time and season of love in the spring. The winter and the autumn, the cold and the rain, which once were in the past have passed, and the coming winter will never arrive. Nevertheless, in spite of the unchanging presentness of all that happens, the poem is not frozen into one situation. Within the firm and steadfast bond between the lovers and the undefined immobility of time there is an astonishing degree of movement. And it is not a movement of external events, even though each of the described events in the poem has its inner repercussion and influence. It is rather that the existential truth of the inner, emotional events is itself the central point of the poem. And this is so for all the layers and all the verses of the Song of Songs. The system of relations undergoes various changes of parting and coming together. Not for nothing are there so many references to dances within the poem itself. Indeed it is a dance song; everything happens in one place and there is movement all the time. The participants in the dance make frequent changes in their positioning to one another, they assume different poses and vary their movements, and all the time they carry on in the same dance.

The basic pattern of the Song of Songs is therefore one of a dance movement. This dance, since it is an expression of the whole life, and actually of the system of the unity of life on various levels, is not at all simple. Just as it contains simple, straightforward details, it also has complex movements and forms in the background, or as a choral setting for the principal dance of the two lovers. The basic movements of the poem, which are fundamental dance steps, can be said to consist of three double forms. The first is manifested when one of the couple is active and seems to move around encircling his partner while the other remains fixed in her place, still and passive. Then there are the sections in which each of the couple speaks, extolling the virtues of the other, and expressing love for her (or him). This is a double form because it is not done only by one of the protagonists: both of them do it interchangeably throughout the book. Another basic form is more dramatic, continuing and quickening the previous form so that there is a certain spatial movement in breadth, a kind of running away and a pursuit, as when one of the couple goes after and seeks the other out while the first hides and keeps running away. In the language of the Kabbalah, while the first form is of the order of face to face, the second form is of the order of face to the rear. And of course this latter form is a double movement, because it is done interchangeably by the members of the couple, in order to emphasize that there is no real flight or hiding, but only a dance movement within an overall design. The pursuit and the search, in spite of being very intense and full of emotion and excitement, do not ever show despair, even for a single moment. The couple are so sure of the bond between them that they never fear for the fate of the love itself. The pursuit and the flight are the cosmic to and fro movement of the universe and represent the complementary aspects of the single process.

The third form of the dance is one of more intensive inwardness, still a dance even though outwardly it may show very little movement at all. This is where the dance seems to shrink to a constricted space, where the movements are scarcely perceptible and there remains only a sort of vibration. Instead of the to and fro movement, there is a *mati velo mati*, a play of being visible and invisible. I refer to the verses when the beloved speaks of her love. Sometimes she speaks about it to others, like the "daughters of Jerusalem," and sometimes she talks to herself. In these verses there is a certain reservation, but within the constraint there is expressed the clearest declarations of the power and enduring intensity of love.

All that takes place in the poem has its setting in a background that is both real and imaginary: Lebanon and Amana, Ein Gedi and Jerusalem. Like the story plot, the setting is not altogether real. None of the places mentioned in the Song of Songs seems to need any verifiability as a specific place. The locations, the trees, and the plants do not carry the authenticity of specific objects in time and space; they seem more like legendary or dream fragments. Even though the poem does not speak of anything that is not of this world, neither mythical beasts nor celestial creatures, and everything appears to be quite real and earthy, there are, nevertheless, features like the vineyard and the apple tree, the daughters of Jerusalem and the little foxes, and even the watchers of the walls and money for the vineyard, all of which become the elements of a dream world. Moreover, all of these seem to be no more than the setting for the dance; they provide a miragelike background for that which is the only genuine reality, the two lovers and their dance.

This relation between the protagonists and their environment is one of the factors defining the deep love that is the essence of the Song of Songs. Also, on the level of individual/personal experience, love can bring about such a feeling of unreality that the world seems to become no more than a painted backdrop to the validity of the beloved.

And of course, these things assume a more profound significance with every higher level of the poem's multifaceted contents. The described reality becomes, at a certain stage, only a series of symbols for other essences on a higher plane. The material existence of the world is nothing more than an ethereal covering for an immaterial world, which becomes increasingly real and makes of the substantial world no more than a metaphor.

As manifested in the Song of Songs, love flows in waves of coming together and parting, whether in the earthly story as a lovers' meeting or as a search for the beloved, or whether in the transcendent aspect of approach—the disclosure of desire and the passionate mutuality of love—or by the distancing—as expressed by a certain hesitance or a waiting for an opportunity, a tarrying for a stirring up of love. The expressions of love's awakening are found mainly in those verses in which the lovers speak to one another and about one another. And these too have their different degrees of tension—there are those that are full of endearment and praise, descriptions of the beloved, and of real encounters and total surrender to the other. And there are, in contrast, the other sides, of waiting, of temporary parting: "Turn my beloved and show yourself a gazelle or a young wild goat on the hills of Bethar" (Song of Songs 2:17). The repeated refrain "Do not rouse, do not awake love until she is ready" (Song of Songs 3:5) would indicate that one should not rush love, that one should wait a while for the right moment, or for the right stirring of the heart, that there is a certain period of time when it is possible or necessary to be apart. And, even more so, there are also times of weariness, of an inner languor, when "I have taken off my robe, how shall I put it on? I have washed my feet, how shall I dirty them?" (Song of Songs 5:3). Such phrases are saying that it is desirable to wait a little, that the hour is not appropriate, because there's something else more important just now. Nevertheless, it should be kept in mind that even in the distancing, when the tension is diminished, there is no questioning the intensity of the love, there is no doubt about the essential tenderness. These phases are fundamentally variations in the normal vibration of life, the waves, rising and falling, of the one immutable feeling.

One of the outstanding elements of the Song of Songs is the active role of the beloved, the bride. Although the lover speaks and is quite vigorously present, the central role and the dominant point of view is that of the beloved maiden who is constantly seeking him out. It is her heart's musings that are given more prominent expression, her thinking about his whereabouts, her talking about him to the "daughters of Jerusalem," and her constant dwelling on the possibilities of meeting him in various situations and places. Of course, all of these have their interpretation on each of the planes of meaning, but it is on the more comprehensive and spiritual level that this emphasis on the bride is important.

The relation from above to below, the love of God for the soul of man and *Knesset Yisrael* and His *Shekhinah*, is a constant and unchanging truth. There are not many variations or hesitations about it, even though this love is not always clearly made manifest. But even when the lover, who represents the Divine, does not speak to us, and even when He himself seems to be at some unbridgeable distance, His love is steady and beyond doubt. The poignancy of the variations in feeling, of approaching and parting, of total devotion at one moment and of hesitant waiting for love to be stirred into desire at another moment, all belong to the beloved who is the human soul or the earthly form of the *Shekhinah*, *Knesset Yisrael*.

The dramatic description of the lover knocking on the door seeking entrance, while the beloved is not yet ready to receive him, idly hesitant about getting up and opening the door, is the classic description of the relation between *Knesset Yisrael*, the soul in particular, and the *Shekhinah* in general, to the call from on high. The lazy heart, the inner reluctance to total commitment, even to any alteration of the comfortable existing situation, are common to both the people and the individual. This great opportunity, that comes to nation and to person occasionally, is often missed. And afterward, the belated awakening of consciousness to the wonder of what was being offered urges one to run after and catch the missed opportunity, in spite of the difficulties, the dark night, and the cruel watchers of the wall. All of this is an intrinsic part of the chronicles of Israel, just as they are intrinsic to the life of any human soul. They are universal depictions of the experience of the almost attained spiritual solution.

A vital aspect of the Song of Songs lies in the verses that do not deal with the love affair and seem to divert attention from it for no apparent reason. Among them are passages like "Look not upon me, because I am black, because the sun hath looked upon me: my mother's children were angry with me; they made me the keeper of the vineyards; but mine own vineyard have I not kept" (Song of Songs 1:6), or the verse "King Solomon made himself a chariot of the wood of Lebanon" (Song of Songs 3:9), or the last part where apparently unimportant matters about vineyards and money are mentioned. The truth of the matter is that these divergent passages, wherein the dance seems to come to a standstill and nothing moves, are the unexplained climactic points of the whole story. The stormy movement yields a place to a quivering standstill, and as the tension rises the silence becomes complete. It is in these passages that there is suggested the conclusion, the meaning, of the tale. If the poem as a whole is a song of desire, of love that, in a certain sense, is from afar, a devotion that is directed to some future actualization in time, these verses speak of a consummation, of a finality and fulfillment, of a marriage after an engagement.

The prosaic tone of these passages, and even their unpoetic style, indicates that perhaps all the rest is only a lot of agitated running about, and that dream and desire do eventually get to a dimension of practical realization. True, this conclusion is never stated outright, because, as said, the poem remains incomplete; there is no ending. But a certain course is pointed out, how after the tormented searching, after the waiting and the partings, there is fulfillment.

14

Ecclesiastes

Ecclesiastes is one of the most complicated books of the Bible. What it says, as well as the way it says it, is packed with difficulties of various kinds. Involved linguistic structures and decimated sentences make it hard enough to understand, but even more demanding are the problems arising from the fact that we cannot always fathom the author's intention. We do not follow the course of the book's progress and often wonder whether it isn't just a collection of isolated fragments rather than a definite way through a profound ferment of problems. Does the book get around to any conclusions (positive or otherwise), or is it all the same vicious circle? "Round and round goes the wind, and on its circuits the wind returns. All the rivers run into the sea and yet the sea is not full" (Ecclesiastes 1:6).

But these complex problems seem to be secondary to the basic question asked by almost every reader: What is the place of this book in the Bible? Why did the sages of the Great Assembly (in the early period of the Second Temple) see fit to include it in the Holy Scriptures? Of course, the final statements to the effect that "the end of the matter, when all is said and done: Fear God and keep His commandments: for that is the whole duty of man" (Ecclesiastes 11:13) are quite proper to Scripture; but they are not enough, in and of themselves, to save the entire book from the impression that its spirit is different and even strange to the rest of scriptural writing.

The explanations that have been given by scholars are not quite satisfactory. Some, for instance, argue that the book was composed by King Solomon and that this was enough to give it weight and authority. But in the Talmud there is a discussion on Ecclesiastes and among the opinions presented are some that were in favor of excluding it from the Bible, while the counterarguments did not claim that the greatness of the author gave it any particular stature.

Also, the contention that Ecclesiastes was included in the Holy Scriptures because it was a very popular book at the time seems to be groundless. It assumes that the men of the Great Assembly, who gave the Bible its final shape, were just putting together an anthology of Hebrew literature—an assumption that is repudiated by the essentially religious power of the Bible. But it is obvious that the selection for Scripture was based on the inherent sanctity of a writing, and if the Book of Ecclesiastes had been considered a secular work, no matter how popular or profound, it would not have been included. For example, the book *Proverbs of Ahikar*, which was widely read at that time, and other such works have slipped into oblivion. Popularity was never a significant factor pressuring the sages of Israel, and certainly could not bring them to sanctifying a book. Consider for instance, the book *Ben Sira*, which was so popular it was quoted for generations even after it was excluded from Scripture.

The only conclusion to be reached is that Ecclesiastes was considered a truly holy writing that fit in with the rest of the scriptural texts, a conclusion that, in turn, demands a revision of the first impression and a more thorough inquiry into the contents of the book.

This first impression, as said, is of great bitterness, a

rebellious rejection of everything; one feels that its spirit is pessimistic, its deductions heretical. But this is only the initial reaction. Further reading leads to a recognition of something else beyond the apparent despair and skepticism. What consistent line of thought lies behind the cry: "All is vanity"?

It isn't a matter of determined heresy, or even simple unbelief; it may rather be regarded as a nihilistic tone, a repudiation, or decimation, of all values. Everything is a target for mockery and scorn, and even if the author of Ecclesiastes does not really hate the world, he certainly has not much use for it; indeed, he clearly despises it. The repeated declaration that all is vanity is not a philosophical thought or the result of any system of reasoning. It's simply an outburst of weariness and disgust, a terrible cry of consuming doubt and despair. And it does not find anything to cling to, nothing seems to be secure from the scathing criticism of the preacher; so that the deprecation of all values leads only to the one heartrending conclusion: "Vanity of vanities, all is vanity."

Nevertheless—does this awful nihilism really strike out at everything from birth to death? A deeper reading of the text points to an intriguing line of discrimination. Ecclesiastes takes everything apart with his weary and penetrating gaze—but it is only the tangible, material world that is so put to scorn. Wealth, wisdom, women, old age and youth, life, and time itself are all vanity; the same fate takes them all and they perish. Death consumes and equalizes everything. Only the abstract or spiritual values, those that are not connected with this world, are exempt from the preacher's scathing.

It is possible that he simply has no relation to absolute values that are beyond the factors of everyday life—or else that his criticism does not include them. The comment of the sages on the passage "there is no profit under the sun" (Ecclesiastes 2:1) maintained that indeed there was no profit under the sun, but that above the sun there was profit. This is close to the spirit of the book, even if Ecclesiastes does not treat matters "above thc sun." For these matters do remain lofty and pure; the sublime is left intact by the preacher. There is profit above the sun. And thus it may be said that Ecclesiastes is a bitter cry of defiance against life in the world, an expression of disgust for the world as it is.

At the same time it shows the worthlessness of the world. (There is, in other words, a higher standard of value than that of this world.) And since the ideas of Ecclesiastes are not isolated and independent notions, their meaning has to be examined within the larger context. To take them out of context would be to invite distortion. In this sense the book has to be seen as part of the Bible. Its ideas have a function in the whole of the scriptural message.

The nihilism, doubt, and pessimism of Ecclesiastes are not intended to assert anything on their own. Their purpose is to serve as instruments for the overall message of the Bible, which is of a very different nature. If we take the trouble to hold the Book of Ecclesiastes up to this more penetrating scrutiny, it will become evident that in certain respects it acts as an introduction to Judaism. It can be a deeply meaningful approach to the Jewish spirit in two ways.

On one hand, Ecclesiastes is a key to a more spiritual

humanity, or at least an expression of the feelings of those who are less driven by physical needs and desires. Its scorn and disappointment with the things of the flesh is based on an annihilation of the three concepts that support materialism. It demonstrates that things change, that all physical forms are in process of constant transformation: it shows that all possession is transient, temporary, and given to time; and it repeatedly points up the bitter mockery of all pleasure. In such manner it supports the spiritual outlook of those who seek the good for its own sake, who choose the positive values of life without expecting reward for it. Indeed, precisely because the world is constantly in transition, without any stability or reliable values, there can be no reward or meaning in it. Ecclesiastes thus speaks for the spiritual foundations of Jewish life, and as such it has found its proper place at the end of the traditional prayer book, where it is chanted and recited aloud at the conclusion of the annual cycle of Torah readings. It is the corridor to, and preparation for, all Jewish creativity after the Bible, whose expressions are much more spiritual. One may well believe that after Ecclesiastes and the contributions of later generations, the Torah became clearer to the understanding and it was easier to perform the *mitzvot*.

Moreover, the Book of Ecclesiastes is a key to a more inward-directed Judaism, posing as it does the great question: What is life? What is it all for? These are the basic questions of every thinking person. And in the course of the book, all the substantial, rational, and usual solutions to this question are demolished, again and again. What is the purpose of life? Certainly not any one of the possibilities that Ecclesiastes raises, telling us of his own experience and his eventual despair. The essential conclusion of the book, in terms of an answer to the fundamental question, is: there is no way of finding the purpose of life within the framework of physical life itself. And if we pursue this line of thought we reach the conclusion: if there is a purpose to life, it has to be beyond life. The final verdict, as indicated by this conclusion, is expressed in the closing verse: "The end of the matter . . . is to fear God and to keep His commandments" (Ecclesiastes 11:13). And if this statement does not constitute an adequate counterweight to the vehement disillusion of the book as a whole, it is only because the fundamental riddle of life remains unanswered.

But if Ecclesiastes poses a problem, what is the answer? Here we may attempt to see the problem in its wider scope, within the context of the scriptural writings. Ecclesiastes is a question, and the answer is the Bible as a whole. True, the book is also a bitter cry, to which essentially there is no answer—as evidenced by its own consistent logic. Nevertheless, the response appears in any number of ways in the other books of the Bible. The closing declaration, "When all is said and done, fear God and keep His commandments, for that is the whole duty of man" (Ecclesiastes 11:13), is after all the point of all the books of Scripture.

The inclusion of Ecclesiastes in the Bible is itself the answer to the question it raises. Thus it is within the biblical context that the hidden positive quality of the book becomes apparent. It leads to an ultimate acceptance, a positive view of life, and serves as an opening to a more wholesome and complete Jewishness. When the bitter tang of Ecclesiastes is imbibed with a certain care, when one adds the solution of the biblical way of life, it becomes a blessing, a healing. For the world is too much with us, and we are too attached to its false conceptions of things. In order to attain anything real, we have to make use of this bitter elixir of Ecclesiastes to cleanse the heart, to purify our feeling, and to prepare ourselves for a higher relationship to all that exists, above and below.

15

The Lamentations of Jeremiah

According to tradition, the author of the Book of Lamentations is the prophet Jeremiah. The Bible itself provides a hint for this, in 2 Chronicles 35:25. But the authorship is perhaps less significant than the time the book was composed. Because the *megillah* is not a collection of lamentations written many years after certain tragic circumstances, it is a very direct reaction to the disastrous events of the years preceding the destruction of the Temple (like the lament on King Josiah, "How is the gold become dim," in chapter 4) and after the destruction. They were written very close to the catastrophe itself and are not the product of a long-distance view with a historic perspective emotionally divorced from the events as they were taking place.

And precisely for this reason, the quality of the *Megillah* of Lamentations that stands out is its enormous restraint. Even though it is a record of the most terrible of events, war and its aftermath, hunger and devastation, political subjugation, destruction of the Temple and Exile, none of these is described in detail, or even in a broad aggregate. Which is not to say that these terrible things are not mentioned—on the contrary, each one does receive proper attention, without trying to cover anything up. And they are described, for the most part, in incomparably savage and bitter terms. In few words and precise phrases the full depth of the tragedy is brought before us. Nevertheless, the book does not attempt to emphasize the horror and the abysmal depths of the disaster. The absence of detail seems intended to dull, and not to excite, emotional reaction. To which feeling of restraint, one may add the stylized form and the careful editing: all the chapters are written in a unified meter and rhythm and (with one exception) are arranged in alphabetical order.

It seems that the reason for this restraint is to be found in the fact that the book is an expression of grief and is not a historical description. The general disaster and the many accompanying horrors are well known. And any attempt to express them more thoroughly would only arouse unbearable pain. A book of lamentations does not need to stir the heart to weeping—the heartbreak is already more than abundantly present. The severe literary form, from the rhythm to the alphabetical arrangement, is intended to enclose and keep the pain in such a way that it could get expressed in some controlled fashion. Were it not for this strict framework, there would be no end to the emotional outbursts. Were the lamentations not fixed in such orderly fashion, they would never be able to come to some termination.

This restraint, the severe literary framework in which the grief was given form, does not lessen the power of this book of lamentations. To a degree, they even add a special force and greater influence. Because there are no horrors specified and what is written is no more than brief and abridged depictions, the reader can supplement the dirge-like descriptions by himself and with more bitterness fill in the empty spaces. The relative scarcity of exclamation marks and words of anguish obligates the reader to develop his own reaction to the things he absorbs. In this respect, the lamentations are only an opening, or an introduction, to the true weeping—the cry of the listener. It is precisely because the wail is not heard loud and terrifying, because it is restrained and orderly, that it is heard so clearly.

Three of the chapters in the book begin with the word *How*. And quite justifiably the book as a whole is called *Ekhah* (how), not only because it is the opening word, but because it is the key word throughout. There is grief and sorrow in the *megillah*, weeping and moaning—but more than all else, there is a series of questions. These questions are genuine queries, even though they sometimes seem like rhetorical questions. They are queries that cry out for the light of understanding—and thereby beg for some sort of solution. There is enormous pain in these questions, but they are not vengeful cries of defiance and challenge. Although they are not given to be answered within the body of the book, the questions provoke a genuine search to know and clarify the reasons for the horrors, to comprehend their significance, and even to find a way to solve the problem, or to get out of the impasse.

Presenting the matter in the form of a question in itself produces a feeling of loss and pain. *Ekhah* expresses the essence of the incredulous—"How could the order of a whole world be shattered and a new reality take its place?" When the sorrow and the agony somehow become a part of consciousness, when the facts of a bloodcurdling reality become tolerable to one's mind, it means that the greatest shock of the catastrophe has passed. A horrible knowledge of the worst kind can be borne by man with all its pain, once he is able to react to it in some rational manner. But there is a stage (whether temporary or lasting) in which the experience and its suffering are not only unbearably painful but are not even capable of being grasped by the mind. It is a wild nightmare, in which no stated facts can convince one of its existential actuality. The question "How can this happen?" does not seek to know the mechanism of the disaster, in terms of its causes and development. The inquiry does not really try to analyze or comprehend it in military or political terms; it is not a request for historic or even moral explanation. The question is a very much more profound and urgent cry: "How can such a thing be?"

Thus, the fact that these laments are repeated again and again every year, and the question "How?" keeps coming up constantly means that in truth there is no reconciliation with the way of things to this day. When the divine poet speaks of the return to Zion, saying: "When the Lord brought back the captivity of Zion, we were like men in a dream" (Psalm 126:1), the dream that he is talking about is not the redemption but its opposite—the Exile itself. The Exile is seen as a long, drawn-out nightmare from which the people will eventually awaken and find itself established in a rational and authentic reality. And so long as this does not happen, the mourner stands before his distorted existence and wonders: *Ekhah*? (How?).

Some of the questions in the book are posed in a general way, without their being addressed to anyone in particular, expressing as they do the mind's inability to accept what is happening. But there are other questions, addressed directly to God. Some of them ask about the nature of the contemporary events, and others are inquiries about the future, what will be. These latter are another aspect of the lamentations. In this sense the lamentations are not only expressions and reminiscences of pain and sorrow; they are outpourings of the heart, conversations of the mourner with God. The Divine presence is strongly felt in every verse whether it is in the form of a direct question to God or whether there is no mention of God at all. To be sure, the names of the actual enemies are recalled as well as their acts of cruelty and horror and their exultation at our distress. Nevertheless they are seen as peripheral factors, mere instruments in the hands of God. It is the Holy One Himself who strikes; it is He Who wounds and slaughters. At the same time, the book does not cry out in bitterness against God, or even complain in self-justification as in the Book of Job, or even in the hurt tones of Jeremiah.

In spite of the awful descriptions in the Book of Lamentations—"He hath bent his bow like an enemy: He stood with his right hand as an adversary" (Lamentations 2:4), "Thou hast slain them in the day of thine anger: Thou hast killed and not pitied" (Lamentations 2:21), and many others like these—it is hard to find traces of remonstration and complaint. And the main reason for this is because there is a deep inner recognition that these punishments are not altogether unjust. Job, who complains about the evil and pain in the world, emphasizes the injustice of it all, that disaster strikes at the deserving and the undeserving, while the *Megillah* of Lamentations does not permit itself such a cry of defiance. The unbearable events certainly occur, but they are not necessarily "wrong, unfair, and wicked." Although the book does not deal much with recollection of sins of the past, these sins are not repressed, thrust away from sight. There is also no heavenly justification for the terrible things that happen to man; there are no statements, as in the Book of Job, on the order of "the Lord giveth and the Lord taketh away, blessed is the name of the Lord." Even though beyond the words of grief there is an awareness that the punishment is somehow just and righteous, that those who suffered had it coming to them. But it does not muffle the agony, the cry: "Behold O Lord and consider to whom thou hast done this" (Lamentations 3:20).

The general mood of the lamentations is interwoven not only with faith in God and in the rightness of His judgment, but also with a deep and even intimate bond between the mourner and God. Not only is the Lord always present, but it is possible, and even a privilege, to weep before Him. The relation to God with all the heartache and suffering is not a relation to the "Judge of the whole earth" or to "King of the World," but to the "Merciful Father." The blows that He distributes are not the blows of wickedness; the sufferings that He causes have a good reason. But the fact that the judgment is just does not eliminate the pain; the fact that the son receives his suffering without striking back does not diminish the suffering. Yet the son knows that he is allowed to cry; he knows that he can put his head in the father's lap, the same father who hits at him, and that he can tell him how much he is suffering. As described in the many dirges, poems, and prayers of the sages, God Himself weeps over the destruction of the Temple; He Himself suffers and feels the agony of those who are stricken. Indeed many of these are more specific delineations of the mood of the Book of Lamentations. And much more than the mourner addresses his countrymen, those who are with him and those who will remember these events in the future; he is really addressing God Himself. It is not a petition, nor even a protest; it is rather an outpouring of the heart, a weeping on the part of one who knows that the chastising father is suffering his pain along with him. As in the words of the prophet Isaiah: "And I will wait upon the Lord that hideth his face from the house of Jacob, and I will look for him" (Isaiah 8:17).

Oddly, the more general and abstract aspects of the *megillah* are mostly to be found in the chapter that speaks in the first person. This is the third chapter ("I am the man"), which seems to be the lament of an individual who tells of the suffering he personally experienced. Many commentators have attributed these utterances to the prophet Jeremiah. However, even though most of the chapter is written in the first person, the lament is not that of an individual. The lament is not that of a particular individual relating his personal tragedy; it is of one who is simply using the first person to represent the entire people. The suffering he describes is the suffering of the nation as a whole, and he is only a mouthpiece. Even the statements that relate to the life of the prophet himself, such as "I was a derision to all my people" (Lamentations 3:14), assume a wider significance within the context of the lamentations and serve as a symbol for the people as a whole.

In this chapter, more than in the others, there are passages not only describing the torments and humiliations, but also reflecting on them. These reflections on the evil that befalls one are varied. There is the theme, which can easily be linked to the personality of the prophet, of patient acceptance of suffering: "It is good for a man that he bear the yoke in his youth" (Lamentations 3:27). What is also stated here, quite explicitly, is that the evil that comes upon the world is not a wrong and a distortion of justice. And here too is expressed, in clear terms, the hope that the evil will not last forever—"for the Lord will not cast off forever" (Lamentations 3:31). There is also the hope that the enemies and those who hate will be punished, even unto their total annihilation. These sentiments are to be found scattered throughout the lamentations, either explicitly or indirectly.

But in this chapter there is clear statement of the idea that the evil in the world, which seems to be a punishment from heaven, is not more than a necessary result, almost automatic, of the sins of man—"Out of the mouth of the most High proceedeth not evil and good? Wherefore doth a living man complain, a man for the punishment of his sins?" (Lamentations 3:38–39).

The themes of the *Megillah* of Lamentations are not arranged in any chronological order or in accordance with any subject matter. There is no historical recital of the consequence of events; neither do the detailed descriptions follow any specific sequence. At the same time there are central themes in different chapters. While the first and second chapters deal mainly with the destruction of the Temple, the fourth chapter concerns itself primarily with the siege and the horrors of hunger, while the fifth relates more to the situation after the conquest of the city and the banishment of its inhabitants. But beyond the details and in spite of the clear and precise descriptions of the horrors, the lamentations in general relate to the predicament of the people after the defeat and the destruction. And in this respect there are three motifs that intertwine: the crisis, the isolation, and the humiliation.

The crisis is actually the defeat and the fall, the sudden transition from a lively, densely inhabited city, from an urban center that exhibits power and security, to the total destruction of everything. The confrontation between the previous condition of beauty and strength and the present devastation is repeated again and again. The crisis was somehow also connected with the belief held by the people of Judah and Jerusalem (as described in the Books of Jeremiah and Ezekiel) that all this splendor could never be demolished. There had been a long history, from the time of David, even if with certain small lapses, during which the city had been spared, even when the cities of the northern kingdom and other monarchies had fallen. Furthermore, there was the faith in the sanctity of the city and the Holy Temple, that God would not let His own city and Temple be destroyed. And even though the mourner is himself the prophet who foretold it all, even for him there is a difference between the logical conclusion of inevitable disaster and the inner feeling that such a thing could not really happen. Thus, after the destruction there is a crisis and an overwhelming sensation of having been abandoned.

The feeling of isolation is, on one hand, national and political—it follows from the great powers and the allied countries having cut themselves off from the defeated nation. And this isolation has its personal aspect, when all around are only enemies and there is no one to rely on or to provide support.

Thereafter follows the humiliation—the humiliation of exile of one who is driven forth to be a stranger and to be abased by all who meet him: "Thou has made us as the offscouring and refuse in the midst of the nations" (Lamentations 3:45). It is, too, the national humiliation of the loss of honor and self-respect.

The Book of Lamentations articulates the sorrow and the agony, but it also expresses hope. And more than the explicit statements concerning the future, such as "The punishment of thine iniquity is accomplished, O daughter of Zion; he will no more carry thee away into captivity" (Lamentations 4:22) or "Turn us unto thee, O Lord, and we shall be turned; renew our days as of old" (Lamentations 5:21). The hope is to be found in the very essence of the lamentations—as a crying out to God. In the very act of turning to the Divine is found the basic source of consolation. The disaster is not the result of some blind, meaningless, and unprincipled force; it is a punishment. And no matter how difficult and unbearable this punishment, it is a part of the Divine providence of His special and specific concern for His people. So long as this complete faith in God and His power exists, there is always the chance for revival, there is always hope.

16

Esther: A Mission in the Harem

The Scroll of Esther is an intriguing and astonishing instance of a miracle that has no supernatural element whatsoever. It has no trace of a *deus ex machina* or of mysterious happenings over and above the events that themselves radically change the situation. Rather, all the motivations, desires, and explanations are plain to be seen. In principle, this is an important key to understanding the significance of the Jewish attitude to miracles. It is clear, at least insofar as something of this nature can be clear, that in Jewish thought the essence of the miracle is not identical with the supernatural event, but is linked to its significance—the content and the result arising from the combination of forces and personalities involved.

Thus, in the Scroll of Esther, where everything is apparently revealed and comprehensible, the narrative is in a certain sense misleading. When we examine the details of the story, it becomes apparent that this is a complex tale, having several levels of which only the edges are visible. Deeper penetration reveals different aspects of Esther's role and even of her being. From the moment of her being taken to the palace, we discover an interesting and instructive phenomenon in regard not only to the sequence of events thereafter but also to their significance.

The fact that Esther had come to live within the palace was not planned, that is to say, she was not an emissary of Israel sent to operate within the king's house. Nor was she the prototype of the beautiful spy planted in the courts of the enemy. However, from that moment, even before she became queen, it is clear that Mordecai had ideas of his own and that his own ulterior thoughts directed Esther's steps. Both Mordecai and Esther were fully aware of the possible importance of her being in the royal house; thus, from the outset, there was a certain readiness for appropriate action, which ultimately bore fruit.

At the time when Esther first came to the harem, neither she nor Mordecai knew what lay ahead. Haman's deeds and influence, his rise to power, were not yet apparent and, indeed, came only later. It is very likely that, in the early stages of Esther's sojourn there, neither his enmity nor his anti-Jewish programs had taken shape. However, as I have said, Esther was preparing herself for, or at least showing an almost inspired awareness of, what could happen in the future. This is attested by the fact that initially she "had not shewed her people nor her kindred" (Esther 2:10). This discretion was not simply accidental, nor was it necessarily a case of self-interest. Rather, Esther was acting here on the express instructions of Mordecai to whom, as is explicitly stated, she was still obedient (Esther 2:20).

There is here no attempt to hide from anti-Semitism in the modern sense. It was very likely that King Ahasuerus, like most Persian rulers, was more or less tolerant of the religions and peoples in his domain. Yet Esther was introduced into the palace in such a way that it was not at all clear to which nation she belonged—an uncertainty that was the first indication of what was to follow. In everything that Esther was to do there was an element of surprise. It is interesting that Haman, himself an interested party, did not discover Esther's Jewishness until after he was powerless to do anything about it; and since he did not know of her origins, it did not occur to him to act against her.

Therefore, the first stage in Esther's becoming the king's favorite did not bring advantages to "Mordecai's people," as the Jews are referred to in the book. It was common in those times for the women of the harem, the favorite concubines who reached a senior position, to be rewarded with a series of benefits and privileges for members of their nation. In almost every culture with a similar social structure that we know of, foreign concubines acted in the interests of their own compatriots or members of their own faith. It was apparently so in the court of the Mongol khans and in the Turkish empire, to give but two instances. In some cases, like China and Japan, preferential conditions for the queen's relatives were a permanent and influential factor in internal politics. There are many instances all through history of the influence of the favorite queen or concubine being of great historical importance.

The fact that Esther, in accordance with Mordecai's instructions, did not overtly seek such "fringe benefits" proves that we have here a case of inspired foresight or, at very least, an awareness of "the sorrow that is to come." There is here an implicit realization of the fact that a representative within the king's court could be more useful if her Jewish identity were not revealed.

Esther is an almost classic example of the conspiratorial connection. On the one hand, she did not disclose "her people or her kindred," even though the king tried various means to extract the secret from her. She actually appeared to be an orphan, someone without relatives, in a way that was somewhat damaging to her status. For, after all, someone without connection, background, or roots was considered inferior. In the long term, this inferior status appeared preferable to the premature disclosure of her origins.

In addition to this secrecy, Esther and Mordecai were in almost daily communication, whether directly or by means of messengers bringing reports to and fro between them. These reports were probably not always important, although at other times they might have been crucial. The single instance recounted in the book concerns a different kind of communication. This is the incident in which Mordecai uses Esther in order to forestall a rebellion being plotted against the king. Here, too, Mordecai's actions go beyond the immediate issue at hand: he had his own reasons for preserving the connection with Ahasuerus, who seemed to him more amenable than other likely candidates to the throne, if only because of his relationship with Esther.

Hence, it seems likely that the Esther–Mordecai relationship went beyond the regular family bond and that Esther was in fact carrying out a mission, whether knowingly and voluntarily or in response to her uncle's instructions. Esther was the unacknowledged emissary of the Jews within the palace. It may be that, from the outset, Mordecai was simply using her to learn about what was going on in the country generally, but it is also likely that he was farsightedly considering of possible future developments.

In fact, Mordecai engineers the high point of the drama: the moment in which Esther reveals herself as a Jewess and reaches the zenith of her political achievements by overthrowing the most important man in the country—Haman. Mordecai not only guides Esther's steps but also encourages her and spurs her on. He shows her that the crucial moment to act has come, even if that act endangers her position and, if the king were so minded, even her life. This was the moment when she must fulfill her task, regardless of the cost to herself.

It is interesting that another aspect appears at this point, which, even if only hinted at in the Bible, seems to be of profound significance: the power of prayer at a crucial moment. Mordecai's prayer is mentioned in the Septuagint—not in the original, but it is still evident from the context.

Esther's feeling that she had come to carry out a great task, her commitment to her people, and her belief in the Jewish way of life and Jewish values are evident when she asks Mordecai to call for a three-day fast to pray for the success of her mission—in memory of which the Fast of Esther is observed to this day. Esther's request reveals not only the strength of her bond with the people but also the extent of her faith in the efficacy of the prayers of the Jewish people and her feeling that she represented their spirit within the palace.

An understanding of Esther's deep commitment to her people changes any initial impression we may have received of her as a woman who, if she did not sell her honor, at least compromised it by going complacently to the palace, losing contact with her past and becoming a woman of the harem. Here, her role was to be pleasing in the sight of the king, to amuse and satisfy him—with all that this role implies. Yet there are other hints of Esther's true character—some very fine and faint, others very clear.

There is the danger she undergoes for the sake of the nation, and her declaration that a day of celebration and feasting be initiated to commemorate the events. This is the act of a woman who has carried out a dangerous mission and feels a need to perpetuate that mission, not only in the deepest social and national sense but also as something of profound significance in her own life. She feels that her deed has value as a sacrifice and epitomizes the many tasks fulfilled for national or ideological reasons.

Into this category must come those tasks, difficult and perhaps among the less pleasant, that women must sometimes carry out to achieve their goal: to surrender themselves totally, while protecting their identity and remembering where loyalty must lie. It is not an easy temptation to withstand. In the case of Esther, she was not involved in a dubious or temporary love affair but actually became the queen, reaching the highest fulfillment of ambition and achievement that a woman in those days could perhaps hope for. Nevertheless, Esther felt that her task was more important, and that it was up to her to represent the Jewish people at this moment. When Mordecai confronts her with the choice between her mission or her rank, her status, and—not least—her life, he makes things very difficult for her. On the one hand, Esther has attained the highest possible position, that of queen, which she was likely to lose at one stroke. On the other hand, if she betrayed her mission, she would be a traitor to her values and beliefs for the rest of her life.

The sages have evaluated a role of this kind in connection with both Yael and Esther: "Better a transgression for the sake of heaven than a good deed which is not." This saying, dangerous to those who abuse it, expresses an understanding of the spiritual dedication that goes beyond mere personal safety and involves a degree of personal humiliation, a renunciation of self. From the point of view of the Jewish woman, Esther's role was not honorable. Had she married a fellow Jew and become a decent housewife in the capital or elsewhere, the feeling would have been that she was fulfilling a *mitzvah* (for the sake of heaven or otherwise) in a perfect, dutiful way. The very fact that she was in the palace to begin with was, in a certain sense, the result of a chain of "transgressions in the name of God."

Midrashic and talmudic literature expands this notion and penetrates deep into the problem of this total devotion. The moment when Esther is required to go to Ahasuerus and use every means of seduction and temptation at her disposal in order to lift the sentence of death that had fallen on the Jews is not just a moment of personal danger. She is required to pass from a passive state to an active one, to become the temptress. Up to that point Esther could still claim that, to some extent, she was in a situation in which she was held under duress. From the moment she takes the initiative in approaching the king to seduce him, she loses her last shred of innocence. Where previously she could feel pure, at least in spirit, she was now to some extent sullied. The step Esther takes when she approaches Ahasuerus with a view to enthralling him with her personal charm is a step more drastic than her induction into the king's harem, a matter in which she had no choice. Consciously, she now decides to endanger not only her life but her soul; and from this moment onward, she becomes the savior of the Jewish people. Inwardly, however, she could no longer regard herself as adhering to the ethical values of her people, not in body and perhaps also not in soul.

Other generations have maintained that, when a man gives up his life while his soul is pure and unsullied, he has reached one level of sacrifice, but that there is a further level, where an individual not only gives up his life but also exposes his soul to a danger, whose result none can foretell. This test of sacrifice—the hidden, unexplained test that is not stressed in the Scroll of Esther—changes this woman from a mere historical figure to a national heroine. The mechanism of the miracle is plainly revealed and visible. All its elements are clearly spread before us. Esther is the woman around whom this miracle revolves, the savior whom we later bless in the religious festival of Purim recalling her act of heroism.

VI

17

The Motif of Light in the Jewish Tradition

Light is the Genesis-creation of the world: the primary utterance of creation is "Let there be light," and the first act of creation is the distillation of light, its separation from darkness. The *Midrash* asks: Where was light created from? And the answer is whispered: "God cloaked Himself in a white shawl, and the light of its splendor shone from one end of the world to the other" (*Genesis Rabbah* 3:4). In other words, light, fundamentally, does not belong to this world; it is, rather, an emanation of a different essence, from the other side of reality.

Light serves as the symbol of the good and the beautiful, of all that is positive. The difference between light and darkness assumes such a general and metaphysical significance, and the advantage of light over darkness is so obvious and self-evident, that it serves as a sharp metaphor: "Wisdom excels folly as far as light excels darkness" (Ecclesiastes 2:13). Light as a positive symbol is so prevalent in biblical Hebrew that redemption, truth, justice, peace, and even life itself "shine," and their revelation is expressed in terms of the revelation of light.

The symbolism of light goes even higher than that: Divine revelation itself is a revelation of light, the *tzadikim* in the Garden of Eden "bask in the light of *Shekhinah*," and even God Himself is "my light and my salvation" (Psalm 27:1). Hence, too, in the language used by the kabbalists, all of reality is "lights" and "enlightenments," all the way up to "the light of the Infinite, be blessed."

This light metaphor is not only an abstract and intellectual one. Light is even personified—it enjoys its own existence—"The light of the righteous rejoices" (Proverbs 13:8). The way in which human beings relate to light, too, is emotional, almost sensual—"Truly the light is sweet and a pleasant thing it is for the eyes" (Ecclesiastes 11:7).

The symbolic meaning of light as an expression of the positive aspect of reality is not confined only to the realm of language. It is realized also in the use of light and lamps as concrete means of expression, which symbolize and point to an essence that contains holiness, in all its different appearances in reality: in holiness and at the Holy Temple—in the sanctity of place; in the Sabbath and festivals—in the sanctity of time; on special occasions—in the sanctity and importance of the event.

The Temple *menorah*, with all of its ornate and extremely elaborate craftsmanship, was not there for any practical purpose: it stood at the *heikhal*, a windowless hall only seldom frequented by people. Yet it was there as a symbol of the holiness of that place, of its relation to light. This *menorah*—"the sun's sphere" (*Yerushalmi*, end of *Hagigah*)—is a sphere of sunlight, which shines *through* the walls and the curtains. No wonder, then, that this meaning of the Temple *menorah* was conceived by the Jewish people as the symbol *par excellence* of Jewish existence (as can be seen in Jewish ornaments from all periods), from synagogue mosaics in the Galilee to ornaments on utensils in the Roman catacombs, and even, in a sense, to the synagogue itself—the place where an eternal candle burns day and night.

The same goes for the Sabbath and festival candles. Initially, the Sabbath candle was lit for very prosaic reasons: to make light for those who eat the Sabbath evening meal, so that they would not spend the evening in utter darkness. But, from the very start, the significance of candlelighting has gone far beyond that. The *Shulhan Arukh* rules: "One ought to take care to make a nice candle . . . and some make two wicks, one for *zakhor* and one for *shamor*. . . ." Indeed, it goes further: "If one does not have enough to buy a candle for the Sabbath and wine for the *kiddush* of the day, the Sabbath candle takes precedence"—so much so that "even if one has nothing to eat, he is to beg for alms and to buy oil and light the candle" (*Shulhan Arukh*, *Orah Hayyim* 263). The candlelight, then, has turned into the very symbol of the Sabbath itself, a sort of "light of the seven days" shining in a sanctified niche of time. And just as the Sabbath enters with a light, so, too, we bid it farewell with a light: the *Havdalah* candle, a torch with which to escort the Sabbath Queen's departure.

Even the festival of Hanukkah, which in the days of the Hasmoneans was celebrated in many ceremonies, has, in the course of the generations, been "summarized," and is now expressed by the Hanukkah candles, in the ceremonial lighting of candles that (daily) increase in number to symbolize how "light excels darkness" in the festival of victory, of purification, of historic upheaval. From here the light spreads farther and farther to every event that has something unique about it, from the festivity of Beit Hasho'evah in the Temple, where they used to kindle enormous torches to light all of Jerusalem, to the firetricks of the Jewish sages of those days, the merry bonfire of Purim in talmudic times, and the bonfires of Lag B'Omer—a light of respect and remembrance to Rabbi Shimon Bar Yohai.

The light of the memorial candle, too, although it is mingled with sadness, expresses a symbolic light —"The spirit of man is the candle of the LORD" (Proverbs 20:27). It is eternity, and not sadness, that is revealed in this light. And against it stand the wedding candles—the torches borne by the best women during the *huppah*—a light of pure joy and hope.

The overall significance of light as an expression of the good and the beautiful is, then, divided into shades and subshades of meaning: the general light of the beginning of creation, a light that contains all of reality, is divided into individual lights, each of which has its own identity, both in terms of its mission and of the emotions that it expresses and awakens. Thus, on the one hand, we have the light of the holy place—which does not even have to be seen, but just to be there. On the other, the light of the Sabbath candles—which is to be used—and the Hanukkah candles—which, while they "are holy, and we have no right to use them, but only to behold them," are meant to be seen by as many people as possible. And the same goes for the messages that these lights convey: glory, the joy of victory, a remembrance of eternity, an outburst of merriment. Of course, naturally, we do not always have a single element in its purest form, since sometimes one event or one light contains a few aspects intertwined.

This multitude of meanings exists not only from the viewpoint of the onlooker. The meaning of every light is embodied in a tangible form in the material utensils of light: the oil and the wick, the candle and the lamp. *Halakhah*, which deals very extensively with all these issues (see, for example, the chapter in *Shabbat*), is the formal means by which the different meanings of the various kinds of light find expression. In its technical fashion, *Halakhah* not only establishes external frameworks for ways of action, but also materializes, realizes, and specifies the contents that were poured into these things. The rule that states that one must not make, for private use, a *menorah* in the likeness of the one that stood in the Temple, exists to preserve the uniqueness of the Temple light, which must have no double, no substitute. The statement that all the candles in that *menorah* were turned toward each other further emphasizes that this light is not meant to illuminate its surroundings, but rather to turn toward and illuminate itself only.

The difference between the single wicks of the Sabbath candles and the braided torch of the *Havdalah* candle is the distinction between a light of calmness, of repose, and of homeliness, and the stronger light of the torch, which, on the one hand, accompanies the departing queen, and on the other, lights the darkness that becomes more marked in her absence. The Hanukkah candles stand in one line to mark and count the days, and the *shamash* stands apart from them to point out that, unlike the other candles, it is there for practical use.

Halakhah, then, is a framework through which the abstract ideas find expression; and always and everywhere have customs and aesthetics completed the picture, according to the tastes of the various times and places. There are also, of course, internal and external constraints, which create forms and patterns of their own, constraints related to materials (fuels, and materials for candlesticks and lamps) and considerations such as the weather, and even bad neighbors. Economic and geographical conditions forced Jews to find different means of expression. The oil wick was sometimes replaced by a wax candle, with all the external changes entailed.

Nevertheless, the meanings and fine points of these

matters have never been lost. The Jewish artisan who created and designed the various light utensils for holy services understood that their usefulness is rooted in their meaning. Their use, and even their beauty, should express the precise idea contained in each one of them. The artist's creative thinking tried to express that idea, and sometimes even add additional layers of meaning—from the *Halakhah* and the *Aggadah*, and quite a lot also from Kabbalah—in order to complete the job.

Yet above all, light is there in order to light. Even the hidden Temple *menorah* was diligently crafted so that its hidden light would be as bright and perfect as possible. In Judaism, darkness has never had religious significance; the curtain of darkness and mist is the curtain of *kelipah*; and to the extent that it does have a role to play, it is, in the words of *Sefer Yetzirah*, the existence of darkness underscores light, emphasizes the yearning for it. Even the secret is the secret of light, as Rabbi Israel Baal Shem Tov said: *Or* (light) in *gematria* is equal to *sod* (secret).

Mysticism in the Jewish Tradition

Jewish mysticism never really became a separate domain of spiritual life outside the religious tradition. This may be due to the fact that the initial revelation at Mount Sinai was holy in such a way that it could never be shaken off. The Torah scriptures, at all levels of their composition, from the Bible to the Talmud and the latest commentaries of the sages, succeeded in retaining and elaborating this experience so profoundly that there was not much room for an emotional mysticism, either private or cultic, to develop on its own, outside of the established religious form.

Nevertheless, at a certain stage in Jewish history (from about the seventeenth century), the religious authorities believed that there was a significant danger in that direction. And in Europe at least, Kabbalah, the chief repository of the mystical aspect of the tradition, was taken firmly in hand. Only mature students were permitted to study it, and carefully preserved texts were left to gather dust and sink into oblivion. In later years (mostly in the nineteenth century) there was another, newer element that helped to suppress the mystical lore. Within the strong rationalistic tendency of the age, many influential people (such as the authors of the most important books of Jewish history) were fiercely antagonistic to any mystical approach and tried to disparage it and even deny its existence in the past. The apologetic mood of the time demanded hiding these shameful parts of Judaism and trying to forget them entirely. The result has been a general misunderstanding of the role of the Kabbalah, and of the mystical experience altogether, in Judaism.

The truth is that the Kabbalah permeates every aspect of Judaism, and the "esoteric wisdom" has been a basic ingredient of scripture, ritual, and prayer. Even many popular expressions, in Hebrew but also in the colloquial Yiddish, have their source in the Kabbalah.

Although a careful distinction was maintained throughout these centuries between the *nigleh* and the *nistar*, between the revealed and the hidden aspects of the religion, it was never a division within the people or within Judaism as conceived by its greatest authorities. The *Shulhan Arukh*, the great work that has become the fundamental halakhic text for all of Jewry, was written by Rabbi Joseph Caro, a sage whose authority rested not only on his very broad learning but also on his many-sidedness and mystic insight. He wrote other books of halakhic procedure and law, exegeses on Torah and the like, and in addition he wrote a treatise called *Maggid M'esharim*, which was certainly a kabbalistic work and showed him to be a man who had mystical experiences and visions. Those of his generation who heard about his revelations were inclined to say that it was the voice of the *Mishnah* speaking from his mouth. To this day, the inspired orders of prayers we follow on the all-night *tikkun* of Shavuot are those of Rabbi Joseph Caro. And one of his closest disciples wrote the famous *Shabbat* song "*Lechah Dodi*," now accepted in all circles of Jewish worship, which is obviously a kabbalistic poem. So we see that the greatest of the halakhic legal authorities was very much immersed in the mystical world of Kabbalah.

An interesting item in Rabbi Joseph Caro's biography is that he was a contemporary of the Holy Ari, Rabbi Isaac

Luria. The two even lived in the same city of Safed. The Ari was the greatest kabbalist luminary, according to whom the Kabbalah was crystallized into its recognized final forms. The Ari wrote hardly anything himself; his teachings were transmitted orally, as were most ancient traditions. We have three short poems from his pen, as well as a legal commentary on a tractate of the Talmud.

All of this is only to indicate that there was never a separation of any real consequence between the daily obligations and open practice of Judaism and the esoteric or mystical aspects of the tradition. They have always been connected. They are simply different aspects of the same thing. In the Middle Ages many scholars leaned almost entirely on the writings of Maimonides and pointed to his Thirteen Articles of Faith as the supreme theological authority. But even in those times there was more than one approach to theology. For example, we also have the more mystical approach of Rabbi Moshe ben Nachman (the Ramban). But since there was no central authority to define a consensus of opinion, the differences—which, as intimated, were never as polarized as modern thinkers believe—were allowed to flourish. It is only since the sixteenth century that there has been a consensus accepted by almost every Jew. If there is a normative Jewish theology, it is the integration of the two (never really separate) approaches—the Kabbalah of the Ari and the *Shulhan Arukh* of Rabbi Joseph Caro.

This was possible because unlike most mystical schools in the world, which somehow stressed their freedom from the constraints of formal religion (even when they continued to remain within it), Kabbalah mysticism did the opposite. It always stressed the vital significance of the smal! ~+

details of the law and the ritual. The kabbalists even added weight and meaning to the formal practices in a thousand ways. And when it came to such issues of theoretical theology as the Thirteen Articles of Faith, they simply put different emphasis on the same words. To be sure, they had their disagreements with some of Maimonides' ideas; nevertheless, they did not let disagreement develop into friction and antagonism. Everything in the tradition was somehow incorporated into the kabbalistic framework with a certain broad spiritual comprehensiveness. What is astonishing, at least to the rational thinking of the Western world, is that there were no great contradictions, that the two modes of religiosity worked together as well as they did.

All the Jewish scholars who achieved any degree of eminence were involved in every world of Torah. The Torah was never considered merely knowledge—as that which one learns with the mind and in which one becomes an expert. As one of the sages, Hillel Zeitlin, said: "In many religions there is the notion of a book or doctrine that comes from heaven. We Jews, however, believe that the Torah itself is heaven." When one is studying the Torah, one is in direct communion with God. One is not just reading or studying or even seeking inspiration. In Judaism we, God and man, are talking together. As it is written in the *Zohar*: there are three things that are connected with each other—the Jews with the Torah, and the Torah with God. We do not delve into the Torah just in order to know something in our past or to learn how to behave. To be engaged with Torah is not just the fulfillment of a commandment, a *mitzvah*; it is in itself being as close to the Almighty as we will ever be.

In the *Pirkei Avot* ("Sayings of the Fathers"), a familiar tractate of the *Mishnah*, there is a statement to the effect that one hour of happiness in the world to come is better than all the life of this world. Such a belief may satisfy the mystical ardor of many religious people. But this statement is followed by another—a very baffling opposite to the first—declaring that one hour of *teshuvah* (repentance) and *maasim tovim* (good deeds) in this world is worth more than all the life in the world to come. This is to say that we, in this world, have something no other world contains: we can come into direct communion with God through his Torah. When we study Scripture, God studies with us, the Talmud says. When we perform actions according to the Torah, we are not separate from Him.

Learning is therefore not just an intellectual tie; the more one understands, the more one is connected. Understanding requires a lot of discipline, of the emotions as well as of the mind. The intensity of all thought and feeling has to be contained and directed. Therefore, too, the Torah has its many parts, allowing for a healthy organic life within the tradition. But as with anything of such an organic wholeness, the parts are also interdependent. A faulty part can put the whole thing in danger of breakdown. If the whole thing is, like one of the modern rockets, a vehicle to heaven, a flaw in any one small component can prove disastrous indeed.

Evidently, then, all the parts of the Torah are essential. They are not just complementary or supportive of each other; they also use different means, different languages, to say the same thing, whether it is *Halakhah* or *Kabbalah*, *Mishnah* or *Zohar*. For example, the prayer book has this formula for performing a *mitzvah*: "To unite the Holy One, blessed be He, and the *Shekhinah*." This is a kabbalistic formula. And it signifies that this union of Divine manifestation is the same single purpose of all our actions, no matter which of the *mitzvot* are involved. The scope of the Torah is always beyond any of its parts. It is always the same and it is possible to approach it, to view it, from many different angles.

Customarily, we speak of the different ways of dealing with Torah, from the explicit to the implicit, from *peshat* (literal meaning) to *derash* (exegesis), to *remez* (hint), to *sod* (secret or esoteric truth). All these simply address the same words of Scripture in four different languages, all of which have the same meaning. One of the methods of study is to gain an understanding of the way these languages change from one form of expression to another, how they change from saying something in poetic terms to those of a story, a commandment, and a kabbalistic idea. Consequently, the common view about mysticism and Kabbalah being a different world from the Talmud is a misconception of the organic unity of the whole. The Kabbalah and the Talmud are different forms of expression, each following its own point of departure.

As mentioned, the religious authorities had their historical reasons—like the tragic event of the false Messiah, Shabbetai Tzvi—for frowning on the study of Kabbalah. On the other hand, there can be no denying the perils of the esoteric and the occult. The common people were simply advised to keep away from subjects they did not know enough about, a little knowledge being a dangerous thing in any field. And as far as Torah is concerned, since it is a live wire connecting us with God, anyone who gets involved without taking precautionary measures runs the risk of being electrocuted.

It was in this sense that Kabbalah used to be considered a field that was not accessible to all. There was a need for special knowledge and sensitivity to be able to enter into the realm of the hidden. When studying the Talmud, it is all too apparent when one does not quite comprehend a passage, because the Talmud speaks about people, animals, the mundane affairs of men. A student can easily discern what he grasps and what he does not. But when studying the Kabbalah—which speaks about *sefirot*, angels, Divine lights, and vessels—the ability to distinguish one's own lack of understanding is far more difficult, so that the subtle danger of misconception is a sad inevitability accompanying such study. All of this is not intended to divert attention from the fact that the Torah, including the manifest and the hidden, is all one. To be sure, it is said that it has seventy faces. Indeed, some sources say it has six hundred thousand faces, because that is the number of souls who received the Torah when it was revealed, and each one has, to this day, his own understanding of it, his own orientation and point of view.

When we pray, saying "Give us our portion in your Torah," it is to let us have the merit and the good fortune to grasp our own private portion of the Torah. For the Torah has so many locks and keys, and each key is individual, each doorway is one's own. A person can be considered very fortunate if he finds the special key, the private door that is his to enter. Too often people just keep wandering about getting involved with other people's keys and doors; they make mistakes and get themselves confused and entangled in points of view not their own. The simplest solution is to be certain that one's connection to Torah exists. If one just lets attention be properly oriented, it is possible to feel that certain sentences in prayer, certain passages of Scripture, have special appeal to oneself; they speak to one. Many Jews will learn these passages by heart, becoming emotionally intimate with certain words that serve them as a doorway.

The same thing is true of commandments. Of course, it is required that the whole Torah be accepted and no exceptions be made. Nevertheless, every individual should take at least one *mitzvah* as a very special commandment to be performed with a sense of particular satisfaction and inner happiness. When, in the Talmud, Rav Yosef asks the son of Raba: "What commandment was your father most particular about?" he is inquiring not only which commandment he kept most meticulously, but also which was most important to him.

In another book, the word meaning observant, careful, particular also means to shine. So that the Talmud question reads: In which *mitzvah* did your father feel most of the light? Sometimes there is something that passes before one like a flash of lightning or a resplendent illumination that lights up one's way. It is that key to Torah that is yours, your way, that speaks to you.

Some people find this key in the realm of intellectual content. Others, in the doing of certain actions, the performance of *mitzvot*, and this has as much meaning for them as the complex idea of the intellectual or mystical experiences of the kabbalist. All lead to the inner chambers of the Divine presence. The point is that for each seeker such a key is the hidden secret of one's destiny; beyond rational explanation, it remains beautiful and personally meaningful for a significant period of time if not for all of one's life. The other side of the same truth is that each one is expressing the same thing, the same melody in six hundred thousand voices. For every person has his own unique voice, even when the song is the same.

If a person is unsure of himself, and wishes to know whether his way is appropriate to him, one of the tests of validity would be to examine its flexibility—whether it can be translated into different levels of the hidden or the manifest, as the case may be. It should lend itself with ease to a variety of expressions. If this cannot be done, if his key cannot open the whole of Torah, it may be necessary to reexamine that key and see if it is not perhaps a delusion. There should be more than one way of getting to any problem of truth. A problem, whether it concerns mathematics or science or spiritual reality, can usually be solved in more than one way. What is essential is that all the approaches should lead to the same correct solution. Some go through the air, some by sea, others over land. All should lead to an equivalent answer, even if couched in different words, even if they sound oddly at variance.

Thus the mystical contents of Kabbalah are not necessarily restricted to *sefirot* and angels and other-worldly forces; they are also in the familiar constituents and motions of the body, in the Bible and the Talmud, in all the many vehicles of the Torah. To be sure, the truth cannot be found in the wrongness of things, in the hidden evil, no matter how deliciously secret, or in any mystery that is at once confounding and soluble. Mystery or mystical experience may simply be the way one sees certain truths. For some people the most revealed of Torah passages is full of secret meaning and wrapped in unfathomable mystery; for others, even the most esoteric wisdom is bright and clear, with nothing mysterious about it. The Baal Shem Tov used to say: The numerical value of *sod* (secret) is exactly that of *or* (light).

All of this is best summarized by the story Rabbi Shimshon of Ostropol, who is famous for his two books on Kabbalah. It is told that he decided one day to write a complete kabbalistic commentary on the Talmud, to explain the secret and hidden meanings of this enormous body of Jewish learning. He made good use of his knowledge of esoteric wisdom and completed the complex work after considerable labor. But being a very holy man, he subjected the book to the test of a dream, *she'eilat halom*, and the answer he got to his questions was that his work was too lengthy and elaborate. He made it shorter and again posed the question. The answer was the same: too long. Again he cut his work down, and again he was told that it was not sufficiently precise and clear. When he had made it as short and concise as he could, he discovered that what he had written was *Perush Rashi*, the accepted commentary on the Talmud.

19

“And His Tender Mercies Extend over All His Works” (Psalm 145:9)

If one is in a good mood and has a window overlooking green fields or even a large tree, it is good to sit and look through the window. With an untroubled mind and a little leisure one can see many beautiful things that make the heart rejoice. A little bird pecking at a breadcrumb on the windowsill is enough to make one feel more connected with the beautiful world whose creatures are so perfect and colorful. One does not have to see the splendor of the peacock's tail; it is sufficient to see the modest, quiet colors of the sparrow and its bright, sparkling eyes and shy effrontery in order to be filled with awe and to exclaim: "O Lord, how manifold are Your works!" (Psalm 104:24). Seeing those little birds build their nests, the leaves moving softly in the wind, and the entire world filled with harmonious silence, the beholder is filled with a calm ecstasy. He feels how true and full is the praise to God for His world, for how He has created everything in the right measure and time, and for how "His tender mercies extend over all His works."

It is good to sit at the window and contemplate God's work in this way; it bestows peace and happiness on the soul. But in such a case one must not, say, look at the newspaper—and not just the crime section listing the murders, rapes, and robberies committed daily, but also other items that do not speak of the deeds of sinful humans. Here there is a story about a plague breaking out somewhere and killing many; or an account of a huge storm that destroyed whole cities and buried both people and their work under the debris; or perhaps a report of an earthquake. And while all of these caused the death of elderly people (who may have sinned greatly), and men and women in their prime (who may also have been evil and sinful), what of the little children and babes in their cribs? What could these little lambs have done wrong? If "His tender mercies extend over all His works," why, then, does He have no mercy on these infants? Why does He not show pity for the innocent babes, these creatures so full of life and the desire to live, who were plucked away so ruthlessly and unexpectedly?

This question is not new. Indeed, it is the ancient question asked by Job, and the even earlier question of our patriarch Abraham: "Shall not the Judge of all the earth do right?" (Genesis 18:25). Yet, although this question is ancient, and no intellectual benefit may be achieved by raising it again, it does not cease to be new, cruelly new, for every person who encounters it, both emotionally and mentally. What difference does it make if generations have already asked this question? For the person who poses this question the mystery is as painful and insoluble as ever.

There is, of course, the answer given to Job, which is somewhat hazy and obscure, and still far from satisfactory. Maybe there can never be a satisfactory answer. Perhaps. Yet we can accept the main point of God's reply to Job, namely, not to question and doubt the Creator's attributes, for He surely has His own reckoning. And if He decides to have a certain number of men, women, and children perish cruelly by suffocation or by plague, He has His reasons. There must be some kind of justification. We do not and cannot understand everything.

Moreover, such events are catastrophes, unusual disasters, which are by no means part of the ordinary, necessary course of life. Earthquakes are not an essential component of life—on the contrary. Life is largely based on the steady course of nature, and in this steadiness there surely exists the famous harmony of Creation. In that case, let us ignore the catastrophes occurring in faraway, foreign countries. Indeed, it is easy for those remote from disasters to distance themselves. Yes, let us desist from questions of "why and wherefore." Rather, let us contemplate the quiet, harmonious world in front of us.

Here is a small, ordinary henhouse—nothing special, just a few hens, of whatever stock. Let us observe them, not constantly, but like a busy person occasionally looking out of his window. The chickens live their lives very peacefully, cackling, fighting sometimes, making a great noise before laying an egg, which then lies in a dark corner of the henhouse. Almost idyllic. Someone walks into the henhouse to take one of the hens, and an amusing, noisy chase ensues until the hen is caught, tied, and respectfully carried out . . . to the slaughterer, of course.

This is no catastrophe, just an ordinary event. This is how the world is: chickens are there to be eaten. The slaughterer slaughters; he surely does it with expertise. The blood is spilled, then covered with earth. The chicken still quivers a bit on the ground—and that's it. It will be duly eaten with great appetite. Few are shocked by the sight of a slaughtered chicken. Few will call it murder. This is the way of the world. Yet it too raises the question: Does this also mean that "His tender mercies extend over all His works"?

Some people will indeed say—No! Slaughtering chickens, even by the best slaughterer and for a *mitzvah*, is a crime, a sin of humans, for which God cannot be held accountable. If the vegetarians are indeed right, and God did not intend chickens to be eaten by humans, then "His tender mercies extend over all His works" only in their natural way, when they live as God intended them to live.

The starlings arrive. The little birds are everywhere, chirping and flying about with much flurry, seeking their food. And in every field there are people banging things and making noises to chase the birds away. A stranger standing at the edge of the field may giggle at the sight of a white-haired woman walking about earnestly and rattling a tin can. But whoever watches this scene more closely does not find it amusing. The people banging tin cans, making weird noises, and chasing the birds away look serious and tired. This is no game, and none of these tired people can see the ludicrous aspect of their actions. The seeds sown in the fields have just begun to sprout, and if the starlings lop them off and eat them, all the toil of ploughing, sowing, and tending the field will have been lost. Those people need to eat; those fields are their life and their livelihood.

It is for this purpose, to protect their own existence, that they chase the birds away; it is neither a game nor a pastime, but a life-and-death issue. No one thinks of what will become of the hungry starlings who fly restlessly from one field to the next. The starlings want to live, so they invade the fields; and the people want to live, so they chase them away. Neither passion nor cruelty is involved, only a cold, obstinate necessity. This evokes, unwittingly, the phrase "struggle for survival."

The struggle for survival. As much as we would like to ignore it—and even though it may not be observed from our private window—it is always there. The sparrow may seem to do no harm to anyone, yet it fears the birds of prey. And the wild beasts always lie in ambush for the herbivorous animals. For they, too, need to live, and they too struggle for their survival—and in this war, blood is shed. This is not the wickedness of humans. This is how nature is; there is always the devourer and the devoured. Every so often, in this much-admired quiet of natural living, come the short intervals (which are usually little noticed) in which one living creature is devoured and annihilated by another. For this is a war in which all fight for their lives, with all their strength and cunning. No one is exempt. Truly, the apocalypse heralds the days in which "the wolf shall dwell with the lamb . . . and the lion shall eat straw like the ox" (Isaiah 11:6–7). But until then?

The struggle for survival is not always accompanied by blood and cries of woe. Indeed, many of its manifestations make no impression at all, such as when the cute and innocent bird eats worms and insects. We may find the latter repulsive, but they, too, want to live like every other creature—and they get eaten, in turn.

The struggle for survival exists not only among living things. Is there a more tranquil scene than the sight of sheep grazing in a green field? But even here the struggle for survival continues, with one animal (a sheep) destroying other organisms (the grass it eats). True, the grass is not a living being and may not feel much. But it, too, has the "desire" to develop, flower, grow, and multiply. Who pays heed to the desire of plants to flower? And is there a big difference between a human being slaughtering cattle, a tiger devouring its prey, a chicken pecking a worm in the dunghill, or a worm gnawing at and killing a plant? Everyone eats everyone else—all destroy and annihilate each other—in fighting for their lives.

This is nothing but a more precise observation of the

same phenomenon. Big animals chase smaller ones, and the small ones look for even weaker victims. Plants spread their roots in the earth, extend their leaves, grab from each other, strangle each other. The idyllic pasture is nothing but a field in which an incessant battle goes on day and night: a fight unto death, the struggle for survival.

This war is neither incidental nor temporary; it is part and parcel of the very nature of things: "The strong survive; the weak perish" is its slogan. How odd and absurd, then, does this very poetic verse seem—"His tender mercies extend over all His works." Is it true? Does it not seem like scornful, derisive, back-handed language, a description that is as remote as possible from the bitter reality of the worst of all possible worlds?

A tough, cruel, ruthless world in which the strong set the rules; a world of darkness and evil—this is what our world looks like when examined closely, with cold, unsentimental eyes. The beauty of the world is in reality the camouflage colors of the various creatures. Its wisdom and good are nothing but hereditary instincts for the preservation of life and for procreation. All is one big, everlasting war, an eternal evil.

Many have indeed viewed the world in this way and have concluded (either overtly or unknowingly) that if these are the laws taught us by nature, then let us adopt them as well! And even those who do not act like this themselves reach the sad, if not bitter, conclusion that to be good is a luxury, an act that contradicts the basic rules of this world.

The assumption that the good is contrary to the natural course of the world and that the world is inherently evil is not new—and it is not even amoral or unreligous: "Therefore this world and its fullness is called the world of *kelipot* and *sitra ahra*, and therefore all the actions of this world are fierce and evil, and the wicked have the upper hand." These words were written by Rabbi Chaim Vital, the greatest disciple of the Holy Ari.

Yet the fact that this world is not the world of the good must not scare men or divert them from doing good, even though in so doing they act against the nature of the world. Good, and the reward for it are "above the sun" (Ecclesiastes 1:9). They are not a part of this world and its set of concepts, but rather are above and beyond it. However difficult and harsh the world may be, man does not have to imitate it. Rather, he must transcend it. This is why he is man.

The question of whether the world in itself is indeed evil and cruel ought to be studied, and as we know, delving into a question often brings the answer. The beginning of our recognition that the laws and customs of this world are essentially cruel evolved by our allowing our understanding to open up and by our abandoning many accepted views and feelings. The simplest and perhaps most natural way of viewing things begins from the self, measuring good and evil by what is good or bad for ourselves. A wider outlook enables us to realize that what is good for the multitude, for the nation, or for the human race is good and whatever is useless to them is bad.

If we adopt this view, much of the sense of evil in this world will disappear instantly: When man slaughters a chicken, it is a good deed (for it is useful for whomever will eat the chicken, and the chicken must not be taken into consideration). We exterminate pests by all sorts of cunning and cruel methods; and the eradication of weeds surely disturbs nobody. Total extermination of these, or selfish exploitation of all the rest, is, accordingly, a good thing to which no one should object or even give any thought. Those who adopt this view, then, may complain about personal ill luck or a catastrophe, but not about evil in general.

The feeling and awareness that the world in general is a system of cruelty and evil comes, then, from a wider outlook, which no longer sees everything from the narrow perspective of the individual and which feels also the pain of other creatures—the starlings, the worms, the grass. This view is more just, since it does not define one kind of creature as useful and good and all the rest as evil. Even if we believe that man is the crown and purpose of creation, that worldview does not have to explain everything else, such as the tiger devouring the kid and the wolf eating the lamb, as happening for man's sake.

This is not mere sensitivity but a much deeper level of thinking. But we can go even deeper than that if we widen our outlook further and see things in an even *less* personal, emotional way. What will we then understand about the order and the laws of the world?

The main issue here is death. All the creatures of the world live and exist only by killing others, directly or indirectly. At the very least, the whole world of fauna revolves either around an ongoing destruction of the flora or on mutual destruction (which does not improve the state of things). Life depends on death; all of existence depends on this mutual snatching away of life. These are the facts. But is our observation not too subjective and too limited when it comes to interpreting them? Do we really understand the issue properly?

Clearly, no contemplation or philosophy can solve the issue of death or serve as consolation for it. Even the most ardent faith in the immortality of the soul is of no use, since the sorrow associated with death is neither philosophical nor theoretical. The pain felt at the death of someone close to us is, in fact, not for the plight of the dead, but rather the bequest of the living. The fear of death and the identification with the dead person fully awaken the desire to live, and the sharpest, deep sorrow, the awareness that the loved one is no longer with us. The deceased is surely not entirely dead: his soul rises to the heavenly treasures and he basks in the eternal pleasures of Eden; but this does not diminish our pain at all. "Cry for the mourners and not for the one that's lost, for he goes to rest and we to sighing," says an ancient eulogist, defining the heart of the problem.

In dealing with death we cannot, of course, free ourselves from the personal feeling involved. But we are called upon to distance ourselves somewhat from the personal view and see things in a wider perspective. Death is a horrible event and will always remain so. But is not its horror a result of our own subjectivity?

Let us try to look at death as a neutral biological phenomenon that neither concerns us nor excites our emotions. What is the biological significance of death? In the life–death scale, death is undoubtedly the opposite of life. But what does this mean?

When a body dies, its soul departs from it. Yet the soul does not die. If there is a soul in the body, and if it is indeed a soul, then it cannot ever die, and it exists forever—in Heaven or in Hell, in the world of reality or of imagination. The death of the body cannot touch the soul, which is a separate and distinct reality. Men and animals die, but their souls cannot die.

And yet the body does die! In what sense does it die? It

ceases to live, but what does that mean? At the moment of death, the dead matter continues to be as it was, with no change at all; there is no material difference between the last moment of life and the first moment of death. Changes occur after death: the dead bodies rot in the earth, or are digested in the bodies of other animals. What does this rotting mean? Rotting is not, by any means, the destruction of the matter that constituted the dead body, because matter cannot be destroyed. It is only transformed, changing its chemical properties or turning into vital energy and, in a certain sense, it exists forever.

True, the form is destroyed. But forms are constantly destroyed. Life is an ongoing destruction of forms, of body cells, of living matter, so as to rebuild and re-create life, matter, energy, and activity. Only inanimate matter (stone or metal) does not go through full transformation of form. And even this perception is not entirely precise, since in almost all matter in all its states, there is inner life, incessant movement, creation of energy and destruction of matter, so that matter continues to exist as matter.

The living body lives, as long as it lives, through destruction and death. It destroys old cells in order to build new ones, it goes through constant transformation; and the more alive it is, the more transformations it undergoes. Growth is one form of transformation; movement, another. Every movement of life is a transformation, a destruction of former life in order to build life in a new form.

A body dies; there is no more life in it. But what does this mean? It means that its matter will now undergo a transformation—a radical one, perhaps—from a certain living creature into foodstuff for another creature. The living cells may disintegrate into simpler elements but will be recomposed into another form of life. Such a tremendous change is quite unlike the ordinary changes in that creature's life. Even so, it is not an essential change: the living form has merely undergone one more change in the endless chain of alterations. The embryo begins in a tiny ovum, a single cell of life that was fertilized. It divides and subdivides, is filled with furrows that become deeper and deeper and turn into empty bundles that gradually are filled with matter, turn into limbs, and continue to alter. Each such change is death and life. The previous form dies, and a new form takes shape from it. The fish in the embryo dies and is transformed into a tailed frog, and the frog in its turn becomes some other monster, a triton or a salamander. Then this form dies and turns into something else: a rabbit, a falcon, a man. This is the resurrection of the dead—not in the ordinary way, but in its precise simple and literal meaning.

And when a body is born, when exactly does it begin to "live"? It merely begins a new series of transformations, a new cycle of life and death. Thus, when the moment of death arrives, it is but another transformation, one of many that living matter undergoes. Now, after its death, it begins to live again, in a different form.

Surely, this sudden transformation frightens us and makes us feel sorry for the sudden disappearance of the previous form, which we knew and loved, and for its substitution by a new form that is foreign and meaningless to us. This sorrow of eternal farewell will never change; it is our subjective sorrow. But apart from our personal, limited emotions, death is but a step toward new life: strange, different, unrelated to us, but life nevertheless, just like the other life that we knew and loved.

Death is terrible, but it is terrible only from our own personal, limited viewpoint, which is attached to certain forms. Let us, then, distance ourselves from our preference for certain forms that are close to our hearts, and try to see things from a place where everything is equally close to us, equally loved by us. Or, in more precise words, let us try to see things from the perspective of the Creator, with Godly eyes.

If we look at things in this way, if we also try to see the world from the point of view of the microbes, of the worms and flies living in the dunghill, of the growing green grass and the animal that eats it, then when a body dies, it is now the property of microbes, worms, and other creatures. Now the form of the dead person, who was so close to our hearts, changes into another, very different, form of life. The microbes and worms, too, die in their turn and in their death they nourish the growing grass; and the animal who eats the grass also gets eaten in due course, and becomes a new form of life in an endless life cycle.

Is this really cruelty and horror? If only we detach ourselves from our habitual viewpoint we shall see that death, the cruelty of the struggle for survival, is merely one point in the cycle of life, the unending cycle of creation and re-creation, of shifting from one form of life to another—in which there is no death at all. This is how our ancient sages interpreted the verse "He shall be our guide even unto death" (Psalm 48:15): He will guide us up and above death, in eternal life.

The strong may overpower the weak, but here there are no strong ones, no weak ones. The tiger devours the doe, but the worms who eat up the tiger are not strong, nor is the grass that is nourished by worms. And the doe eats that grass. There are no weak or strong here, only a long cycle of life, no cruelty, but rather a transformation of familiar forms into new forms, new lives.

We can, perhaps, now read what sounded like a mockery—"His tender mercies extend over all His works"—with a slightly different emphasis: "His tender mercies extend over *all* His works," over all of them equally. Unlike our limited capacity for mercy, our limited worldview, He feels endless mercy for *all* His works, which change form but do not lose their spiritual contents—their souls. The forms give birth to new souls. The forms die and are reborn. The dead live and are created anew.

We may gaze outside the window in a melancholy hour, see the green pasture, and know that life in it is not as quiet and idyllic as we thought it was. It is much more complex, sad, constantly changing, but it continues infinitely; forms are forever re-created and reborn. The Holy One be Blessed renews in His goodness daily—nay, at every moment and second—the act of Creation. And we may look at and contemplate many a sad thing, and gaze through the window, even today, and realize that "His tender mercies extend over all His works."

VII

20

After the Bright Light of Revelation: A Conversation with Rabbi Adin Steinsaltz

Q. Since the Jewish tradition is one of the oldest in human history, it would be valuable to learn something of its origin and durability. Is it possible to ascertain the sources of this tradition? Are they specifically Jewish or are they not also drawn from a broad ancient prehistory, like the stories of Creation and the Flood, original monotheism, primitive worship of the heavenly bodies?

Steinsaltz. Even though much of the biblical tradition relates to legends and events that occurred before the giving of the Torah, this total Revelation at Mount Sinai stands at the center of the world of Jewish consciousness. All the other sources that presumably preceded it, like certain stories of the creation of the world, the origins of the laws and customs of ancient society, and so on, did not reach Judaism independently; they passed through the great filtering of Divine Revelation at Sinai. The influences of the outer world, ancient legends and lore of the nations round about, certainly spread to the Jewish people of the time, but it was all cast into the melting pot of the Jewish tradition itself. The bright light of revelation of the Torah at Sinai fused it into a single entity. It was a process that was repeated in subsequent generations. To the extent that external influences did find their way into Judaism, they almost always appeared as subsidiary, not intrinsic to the core. And indeed there was

---

Conversation with Yehuda Hanegbi, *Parabola* 14:2 (Summer 1989): 95–102.

a certain opposition to them; if they could not be merged, they were ultimately ejected. When they did melt into the Jewish tradition, they were so thoroughly integrated that it would be almost impossible to identify them as foreign.

Q. What is the role of Divine Revelation in Judaism, especially considering the preponderance of law and custom?

Steinsaltz. As we have said, theologically and not only theologically, the Revelation at Mount Sinai is the core of Judaism. And this not only because it is the beginning but because it is apprehended as a total and all-inclusive revelation. That is, this revelation is considered the opening point, the transition point, between the higher essence and the lower essence—between God and man. After this revelation there is actually no need for a new revelation because besides being the first or original of its kind, the Revelation is a one-time event that includes all the other revelatory events. It has been compared to the primordial act of the creation of the world, which was also a first and single act and included all that was and will be in the world. So, too, the Revelation at Mount Sinai is such a unique event containing in it all that afterward will ever be made known about the connection between God and man.

Therefore the Jewish tradition is full and complete—not because it relies only on an ancient single source, the Bible, but because it is open to additions. All the accumulated oral traditions are considered part of the original written Torah. Even details of the oral Torah, obviously belonging to a much later period, are considered to be continuations of the original revelation. It is all the same revelation, written or oral, and includes the ancient text and the ever-changing unwritten social form and custom.

In *Pirkei Avot*, the tradition is described as a *Shalshelet Kabbalah*, a chain of reception, a process of handing on, from one generation to the next: from Moses to Joshua and from Joshua to the elders and from the elders to the prophets, until the last of the sages. This concept of a continuous chain is central to the whole Jewish outlook on tradition. And it does not only go back to Revelation. The very notion of the inspired person or persons who act as a link in the chain throughout the generations is a profound contribution to the Revelation without necessarily changing it. The original revelation contained all that was eventually relevant to it. Those men who contributed to knowledge were in reality discoverers; they did not invent new ideas or theories—they merely uncovered truths that were already there.

Q. What is the secret of the tenacity of the Jewish religion, outlasting persecution, dispersion, the fall of civilization, and even the influence of modernity?

Steinsaltz. There are certainly many reasons for the lasting existence of the Jewish religion. In a certain sense, it is one of the riddles, or permanent secrets, of the reality of things. As the philosopher Kant is believed to have said: There are two proofs of the existence of God. One is the stars in the sky; the other is the existence of the Jewish people. One may discern that there is a secret here, a hint of the dialectic interrelation between tradition and historic reality, because when tradition is all-embracing, beyond the influence of time and place, it becomes that in which reality is contained. If and when a collision does occur between tradition and unanticipated aspects of changing realities, the individual person will reach out to find in his tradition those elements of coherence and certainty that are relevant to the new situation, whether it be a material or spiritual challenge. And the Jew has known a great number of such challenging confrontations: exile, servitude, harsh decrees, antagonistic opposing philosophies, and oppressive circumstances. His return to tradition has taken many forms; it was never the mechanical restoration of a fixed structure. The tradition itself adjusted to the new situation. New responses were elicited. This is because the Jewish tradition is not an inert inheritance; it is like a living organism able to react and respond to a variety of changing circumstances.

Q. How does the concept of *Knesset Yisrael* function in the preservation of the tradition? Is it as a mystique of the national ego or as a mystique of egolessness (contained in the concept of the *Shekhinah*, or spirit of God), which is its counterpart?

Steinsaltz. In many respects, tradition in Judaism is called Torah. And this is one of the words that have no exact translation; the accepted translation, law, is certainly incorrect. Torah, even in its verbal meaning, includes the Bible as well as the law, philosophy, dream, legend, and everything else that constitutes human life. The one word, Torah, signifies that which instructs and enlightens; it is much broader and more dynamic a concept than simply the teaching. And the subject of Torah, that which carries it, or the medium through which it is manifest, is *Knesset Yisrael*. The translated concept is "the assembly of Israel," but it is not at all a statistical totality or a numerical sum of a particular group of people. It is that which one may loosely call the soul of the people. Most important is its function as the bearer of the Torah. In many ways its life and actions are themselves among the creative forces of Torah, of tradition. The Jewish community keeps determining *Halakhah*, doctrine and custom, at every crossroad. The decision is made by consulting the Torah and then itself becomes Torah, so that *Knesset Yisrael* is not the passive bearer of a yoke of Torah and law that has been thrust upon it—it is an active component of the Torah. Its entire being is a constant merging of life and Torah and the result is the essence of Jewish tradition. Not in vain has the relation between God and *Knesset Yisrael* been likened to that between man and wife. From this it may be understood that the interaction, besides the love and respect between them, has a great depth of intimacy and potency. In order for something to be born, for anything to happen, the role of *Knesset Yisrael* is that of the bearer, the means, or the vehicle. As such *Knesset Yisrael* is the many-sided subject and instrument of Torah and Jewish tradition.

Q. Can one say that Judaism has a special relation to time, enabling it to transcend the natural forces of decay?

Steinsaltz. The problem of the relation to time is indeed intrinsic to the tradition, but not in the sense of a fossil, of something petrified. Time itself is an entity within the tradition. The image is generally that of a tall tree, a living organism: the more time passes, the taller it grows. The tradition thus does not undergo drastic changes; its essence remains the same. Like certain trees, thousands of years old, that live as a biological unity, the tradition creates from within itself the parts that renew its intrinsic form. The factor of time, as a process of decay, has relatively little influence on its basic essence. It can be uprooted only by some massive upheaval, but not because it has reached a certain point in time. Unlike anything fabricated or man-made, it has the capacity of restoring itself by division and multiplication and growth, and by a stubborn retention of essence.

Q. What are the modes of transmitting the tradition? Is it mainly through written works like the Bible and the Talmud? Or are other factors, such as custom, holidays, and oral transmission, more important?

Steinsaltz. When the tradition is vital and active within the community, it carries on almost without words, without saying anything. It is transmitted because the Jewish tradition is not only a verbal deposit; it is a very inclusive message that relates to the whole of life and not only to religion or to the historic past. Therefore it is passed on via almost all the channels of daily life. The written past of the tradition lives within the details of contemporary work and food and blessings. One may even define the tradition as being composed of two elements: One is that of life—habits, speech, and manners, from the preparation of food and the choice of garments to the various rituals of passage and the facial expressions of the people. The other is that which is transmitted by written texts and verbal teachings.

The relation between these two aspects of the tradition is, on one hand, a very conscious application and carrying out of the inherited legacy. On the other hand, it is an unspoken belonging to the written Torah. That which is not articulated is not less important. The conscious and the unconscious transmission proceed together to create the wholeness of living tradition. And wherever there is a crisis in any one aspect of transmission (if the conscious community connections are severed or if there is a break in the educational conveyance of the past), the tradition tends to become atrophied into some kind of mask of itself, or else it becomes excessively vulnerable to outside influences without even knowing what is happening.

In a community that manages to live in some sort of integrated wholeness, there is a dynamically proportional relation that is not the same for all the members of the community. The functions are divided. For certain people the conscious component is greater; for others it is much less. For all of them, however, there is a need to combine the two components, the conscious and the unconscious, so that the society finds itself automatically structured by them. There is an ordering of functions, as in a living body. The brain, which consists of the more intellectual and learned part of the community, has to be maintained at a high level. The rest of the body, whose level of consciousness is different, divides itself, and each part relates with great plasticity to the rest of the being. To be sure, it is impossible for any part not to have some degree of consciousness or connection with consciousness. At the same time, there is no part without its relatively unconscious physical elements of existence, blood vessels and bones and flesh. The whole is what makes each part function.

Q. As far as the documentary evidence shows, the Kabbalah was never a prominent feature in the life of the people, yet there can be little doubt as to its profound influence on the religion, customs, folklore. What was its place in the past? What is its role today?

Steinsaltz. The Kabbalah was never a conspicuous part of the daily life of the Jewish people. To be more precise, we would say that the Kabbalah as a conscious study was restricted to a small elite. This was usually a closed circle of people who could devote themselves to it—not only because of the intellectual complexities of the Kabbalah, but because, more than in any other field of Jewish tradition, a very great moral purity was required of the student. Such a high level of moral and spiritual experience could scarcely be expected of an ordinary person. In any case, by its very nature, the pursuit of esoteric wisdom is limited to a chosen few.

Nevertheless, the Kabbalah has had such a profound influence on the tradition that one may even see it as the theology of Judaism. This is especially true of the last five hundred years or so—in spite of the fact that in our own time the Kabbalah is just beginning to emerge from the obscurity into which it was thrust by enlightened rationalism. What is apparent, however, is the influence of the Kabbalah on almost all the features of daily life, from ancient times to the present. True, not everyone is aware of it, but almost every Jewish custom is likely to have some kabbalistic significance or at least to have been fashioned by some such influence.

This means that the practical Kabbalah—not in its crude magic and miracle-making folk expressions, but in its deep penetration into the action, rituals and prayers, ws, language, and customs of the people—is still existent. ere is a core of those few who have made the Kabbalah a source of inner transformation and esoteric knowledge. But there are widening circles whose authority was never significant but whose influence manages to be felt somehow. To be sure, only the inner circle is likely to know the meaning of many of the old expressions and actions. In the further circles, people simply know that this is the way things are done; certain words are said, ritual actions are performed without comprehending why or how they came into being. From this point of view, the Kabbalah is still very much present—even if unknown to the majority of the people. Most Jews would probably angrily reject the notion that many of their traditional modes of expression are "kabbalistic."

Q. What lies behind the various legendary versions of the carriers of the tradition in every generation, such as, for example, those mentioned in *Pirkei Avot*, or, in another sense entirely, the thirty-six hidden *tzadikim* (wise men) whose existence sustains the world?

Steinsaltz. The tradition of the *Shalshelet Hakabbalah*, the Chain of Receiving, is basically the tradition of Jewish leadership. It is a listing of a certain number of the more prominent persons who were bearers of the light of knowledge; it does not deny that there were others who also carried it. The point of the chain is that there was a continuity, an uninterrupted flow.

We also have the concept of the thirty-six *tzadikim* whose existence sustains the world from one generation to another. In this age-old tradition, it is not a body of people who are in touch with one another; each one is alone and for the most part does not have any idea about himself or the others. They simply do not know who they are or what they're doing. The important thing is that, from the point of view of Divine justice, the world cannot continue to exist except if there are a certain number of persons who justify its existence. As an archetype, we have the story of Abraham and the destruction of Sodom and Gomorrah. The question is: Why should any place that is full of wickedness be allowed to perpetuate itself? And the answer is that a minimal number of righteous persons can compensate for the evil of the many and check the course of retribution. Thus, if there were not a certain number of *tzadikim* who justify the continued existence of the world, the world would be destroyed like Sodom, like the world at the time of the Flood. Therefore there is the tradition of the thirty-six saintly persons whose existence on earth in every generation, whether they know it or not, keeps the world from being annihilated.

Q. Can there be said to be a definite Jewish body that carries the tradition, whether national, racial, or social?

Steinsaltz. Even in the distant past, there was probably no single body to which one could point as the sole bearer of Jewish tradition; but let us return to the analogy of the body. Generally, we can claim that the center of consciousness is in the brain. But at many periods of time during the day or the night, the point of consciousness moves to different centers. Sometimes it's at the speech center; sometimes it is concentrated in the eyes or some other organ of perception. The movement of consciousness seems to be one of the signs of life and one could almost imagine light bulbs going on and off all over the body to indicate where awareness is being focused.

Every part of the organic wholeness, which is both the mystical and the material body, has a special function that is his and only his. His role is vital to this body and no one else can fill it. And the way a person fills his role is significant, not only for himself but for the entire body. What is more, just as a person cannot be sick only in his little finger, and just as any sickness of a part imperils the well-being of the whole body, so too is there a vital interrelationship between the individual and the community. The way the individual Jew assumes his rightful place in the organism determines the shape of his life and the life of the whole.

Historically, too, there is such a movement of the center of Jewish consciousness, from country to country, from place to place. Of course there have been occasions when the center was not in any one particular place or country but could be seen as scattered, or existing simultaneously in a number of places.

Q. How much of the tradition can you guess has been lost?

Steinsaltz. From the very nature of things, it is very difficult to know the quality and the value of whatever got lost. In those instances where fragments have remained we can only surmise what had once been there, like the stump of a tree. But even less than that can we know anything about human traditions that have left no mark. And this is true of every realm of human life—law, custom, mysticism, art.

In recent generations especially, the wanderings (and changes) of the Jews have been characterized by a brutality and swiftness that are almost unprecedented. We can observe how, before our very eyes, the inability to permit adequate transition and acclimatization of well-established structures (education, religion, social services) and of life patterns in the family has entailed the loss of thousands upon thousands of details.

In spite of efforts to save some fragments of the tradition, most of it is irretrievably gone, and it does not matter whether it's old songs or ancient wisdom or the food preparations of a millennium. A large part of the Jewish tradition is thus continually being lost; and it's not only that most of the old ways and social forms and institutions are being swallowed up by more modern methods—it's the tone and inner unity that go.

To follow the metaphor of the tree, one would say that the whole or branches of the tree had been cut off by a combination of many outside forces. But there is always the hope that when circumstances change, some of the buds that have always remained will grow again—with the renewal of those branches the form and the content will be complete.

In the large scheme of history, it may be observed that the Jewish people, which grew up and reached a certain maturity in its own land, was in exile for hundreds of years. And this meant the loss of much more than national sovereignty; whole areas of tradition were abandoned and only vague hints survived in memory. One can hardly reconstruct the richness of this tradition from the written evidence. To a degree, the temple, the legal and social structure, the schools and synagogues can be pieced together in some fashion or other. The mystical traditions are far more elusive to the modern researcher. Most of them have been totally wiped out by time, such as the schools of the prophets. We have nothing resembling such schools, either in Israel or in the Diaspora. In fact, there have been attempts to make such a restoration by pasting scattered indications together. Some of this material has survived only in written form; most of it is considered irretrievably lost. Nevertheless, the dream or hope of restitution has remained. In the days to come, a regeneration is possible, if the right stimulant appears. This anticipation is possible because, as in every organic entity, the code of the whole is contained in the fragments, so that from the little that has come down to us it may be possible to reconstruct a semblance of the ancient tradition.

Q. Can you point to something definite that has been learned by the Jews that would help other traditions now in danger of extinction?

Steinsaltz. There is at least one thing that other traditions can learn from the Jewish experience, and that is that a tradition in itself—even if it is almost hermetically sealed, something that doesn't exist any more, cannot continue to exist only by the force of inertia. A tradition cannot leave things in a state of unchanging status quo. In the Jewish experience this factor has been very prominent; the group awareness was always alive to whatever threatened it and ready to invest energy to guard the tradition and to maintain it—not necessarily to freeze it. Whenever the group was unwilling to pit itself against imminent change by investing thought and effort, the change was destructive to the tradition.

The question here is not the value or the resilience of the tradition, but the fact that any social form that does not keep reinvesting energy into its continuation will tend to die out. The efforts required are always very great. True, many traditions have survived in conditions of relative isolation. But today, folk cultures are being destroyed by no more than superficial contact with some outer influence. And this is because the people involved are without adequate consciousness of themselves or without the will to do anything about it. They are not prepared to invest the enormous effort required to meet the challenge of the contact with alien forces. But this has to be learned—and sometimes it comes too late.

The Jewish world has almost always been intensely aware of the problem. And over the centuries, a very great deal has been poured into education, in the preparation of spiritual guides and teachers of all sorts, and in the maintenance of the general framework of the tradition. In many places it amounted to one third or even more of the general expenditure of the local or national body. This was one of the main factors that helped keep the tradition going in spite of very difficult external conditions. Therefore, one can say that any group or tradition that is willing and able to invest considerable effort in maintaining its existence is that much more able to withstand the process of decay from within and destruction from without.

The Command Is to Hear: An Interview with Rabbi Adin Steinsaltz

Q. The call is a very great mystery. Could it be said that God's call is a call to be here, present, in the moment? Is this why Abraham, Jacob, Moses, Isaiah all answered the voice of God with the same words: "Here am I," "I am here," as if the call was meant as a call to *be*, to be the "I am"?

Steinsaltz. The "I am" is sometimes as if you were answering "Hello" on the telephone. To a great extent, "I am here" just says "I am listening." The call is directed and not directed; it goes everywhere, in every time, and never stops—but most people don't hear it. When you hear the call, you say, "I'm here." Just imagine a person sitting on a star, sending messages to other planets; he's sending messages over and over. Now what will be the breakthrough point? The breakthrough point is when there is *any* answer. When at the end of nowhere, somebody answers.

Q. You mean the voice is always sounding?

Steinsaltz. Yes, but we are not listening. It even says so in the Bible. It is written that the voice on Sinai was a mighty voice that did not stop. Many years later this is repeated in much of the hasidic literature, that the voice giving the Law, the Ten Commandments, never stopped. It is still giving the Law, for ever and ever, for eternity. Put in another way, there is a very clear message that is always being trans-

---

Interview with Jean Sulzberger, *Parabola* 19:1 (Spring 1994): 26–33.

mitted. The thing that has changed is that we are no longer listening.

Q. And the command is "Hear, O Israel."

Steinsaltz. The command is, first of all, to hear. If you don't hear the *Shema Yisrael*, where are you? So you must first hear. Now, if you are listening, and answer, "Here I am. I am listening," then perhaps a message can come through.

Q. The Talmud says: "If you listen below, you will deserve to hear from above." So is it a question of our attention?

Steinsaltz. Yes. It is a question of our attention. I once wrote about it. There's a saying in the Talmud that there are voices that are so resonant, they should be heard all over the world. One of them is the voice of a woman giving birth, and another is the voice of a snake getting out of its skin. These voices should be heard, but why aren't they? Because the voice of Rome, the voice of the big, busy city, has so much power, it obliterates them.

Q. But what of a heavenly voice?

Steinsaltz. It's what I'm saying. The voice of Rome obliterates almost everything. So the real point is about listening, not so much about the voice.

Q. When the voice calls, why is the name always repeated? God says "Abraham, Abraham," "Moses, Moses," "Jacob, Jacob." Is there a meaning to this?

Steinsaltz. I suppose that it's possible that one time is not enough. It is like shaking somebody who's asleep. At a deeper level, the double call is uplifting, causing the person to move from one level (the name) of his existence to a higher level of the same person. In the Bible, in the first prophecy of Samuel, he hears a voice, but he thinks that it's something else. He needs to wake up. The waking up is a process, and it's a process that has to go through different levels. On one level—again, a quote from the Talmud—"Every day there is a voice coming from Mount Sinai that says 'Repent, errant children!'" Now the Baal Shem Tov is quoted as saying, "There is a basic question: If there is such a voice, why don't I hear it? Or if it is a voice that is not heard, why say it?" And his answer was that those thoughts that come to a person from nowhere somehow call him to repent, to change something in his life. These are the echoes of the voice.

Q. Can the hearer know whether the voice is the voice of God, or whether the voice is the voice of an angel?

Steinsaltz. This is basically what I would call the human problem. You see, the Divine problem is to call. The human problem is to know who is calling. You find it throughout the Bible and later, the constant question: Whose voice is it? Some people think that the mere fact of having a supernatural parapsychological experience is meaningful. But such an experience is just that: a parapsychological experience, and that's the end of it. Merely hearing voices does not mean that one has heard the voice of God, and that is always the big temptation and the downfall of quite a number of people. There are some who are cheats, meaning people who never had an experience, and are just imitating. But there are many people who really heard something, and their very big mistake was that they didn't identify the voice. There is another biblical quotation: When Gideon has his experience, he hears a voice and he says, "God, how shall I know that *you* are speaking to me?" This is in many ways the most pertinent question. "Give me a sign that it is You who are speaking to me" (Judges 6:17).

Q. It's an accepted teaching that Muhammad was called by an angel, not by God. What is the role of angels?

Steinsaltz. We usually say that it depends on the degree. Some people hear a voice directly. Some people hear a voice of an angel. And some people don't even hear that. You know, in Jewish parlance, we speak about something that is called *bat kol. Bat kol* means an echo, but it is not an echo of the mountains. Translated literally it means daughter of a voice. You don't hear the voice itself; you hear only the child of the voice. You don't hear the origin of the voice; you hear it only on the second level. In the Book of Isaiah, in one of the prophesies about the future, it says, "And you shall hear a voice behind you, telling you go left or go right." Now this is a voice, but some people don't hear it. They hear what they call an echo, a daughter of a voice. It was again written that in the time of the First Temple, people got calls directly. The prophets of the time of the Second Temple all talked with angels. Later on, we don't hear the voice any more; instead, we have the *bat kol*, the daughter of the voice.

Q. And that becomes—again, according to the Talmud—the sole means of communication between God and humans.

Steinsaltz. Yes, that is the sole means of communication, which is directed to a single person or to many people. Sometimes this echo becomes thinned.

Q. How do you prepare to receive the echo?

Steinsaltz. Having the call at this level is a very great achievement, even if you hear the echo—even if you hear, so to speak, the echo of the echo. In quite recent times, there was a hasidic rabbi who said that in order for a person to be not just a leader, but a guide of people, he has to have *ruah hakodesh*, a holy spirit. He added that at least he should have an unconscious holy spirit. According to this rabbi, some people have a kind of a clarity of vision; they know how the vision comes and what it says. There are others who don't have that clarity. What they will see doesn't depend on them; they are, so to say, guided unknowingly.

Q. There are many different ways that the call can be received: an angel spoke to Jacob in a dream, Ezekiel felt a hand on his shoulder. What are the different forms the call can take?

Steinsaltz. We never know. One also has to remember that not everyone who has been called is telling us. Sometimes people get not just a call, but also a message. Sometimes the call may be completely personal, so it's nobody business. How the call comes, from the descriptions we have received, is by means of what it is that makes a person attentive. It can be visual or auditory. It can be tactile, or it can be any other way that the person has of knowing.

Q. What is the effect of the call? Does a change, an awakening, a reorientation occur?

Steinsaltz. I suppose that most of these calls, like God's appearance in the world, leave it for me—for the other side—to act. And usually, I don't think that the call really changes what I would call my free will.

Q. But surely when one feels something from above and is touched by it in some way, one must be changed.

Steinsaltz. Even when there is a change, it depends on how deep and how clear the message is. As I say, sometimes it comes loud and clear, sometimes it comes in a much more clouded way, and sometimes a person doesn't even know. A person may receive a very clear message without knowing it; sometimes events, life, or things converge upon a person, but that person doesn't recognize that he is being called. You may have more than one call. Sometimes the call comes not through any kind of a voice; sometimes the call comes because you are put into a position in which a choice is made for you that you never imagined. It may begin with anything from an accident to a disaster. And it may come through a chance meeting. Sometimes you ask a question at large, and you receive a very clear answer when the person who answered it, who was the instrument for answering it, didn't ever know that he was giving you an answer. So what I'm saying is that the change, whatever the change is, seems to be that there is something that I now know. I know at a certain level that I am being told something. What I do with that knowledge is a completely different thing. It could even be that I will ignore it.

Q. There's a whole history of people who refuse the call. Jonah fled.

Steinsaltz. Yes, people refuse the call in different ways. Somebody said a prophet can refuse the call, but he will pay for it with his life. In Ezekiel there is the parable of the watchman who has to warn the people. Now, what happens if he doesn't give the warning? If he tries to flee, or tries to ignore it, later he may pay for it very heavily.

Q. At the same time that God is addressing us, we are addressing God. Is prayer our side of the dialogue, or is there something else?

Steinsaltz. Well, prayer is clearly meant to be something like this. I'm very busy these days finishing a book about the *Siddur* [prayer book], a big book that will appear in English. One of the things that I say is that prayer is basically a kind of very direct talk. Prayer is "I am telling You," and this is something that changes. Some prayers or blessings are just a few words saying, "Thank you. I just want to say thank you," nothing else. In some prayers, I ask something. In others I just complain: "It's not just, it's not fair. You dealt with me wrongly." All of these are prayers, and they can range from a feeling of bliss to a feeling of extreme anger.

Q. When we pray, who is listening?

Steinsaltz. The fact that God is listening is no wonder. We want also, from time to time, to get some kind of a sign that our prayer has, at least, been received. I remember this feeling. It is like the times that I've been left alone in a radio booth. The people trust me not to botch it, so they go out for tea and leave me alone to broadcast. Then I feel: I am talking; is anybody listening? I want at least to get some kind of a confirmation that somebody is listening. As there is a command from the one side—*Shema Yisrael*, "Hear, O Israel"—so there is a petition from the other side in the Book of Psalms, or the prayer book—"Hear me. God, hear me, listen to me." I want to know that somebody is hearing. As it is, except for perhaps a few people throughout history, nobody has this kind of an immediate response, the feeling that the message has been received. I'm not speaking about being answered favorably. I'm speaking about the message being received at the other end.

Q. How can we be better receivers?

Steinsaltz. We are not always well equipped for receiving. I hear a call, and I'm not equipped. Let's take this room, for example. On a completely physical level, this room is full of voices and images. If I have a radio receiver I'll hear voices, and if I have a television receiver I'll see images. So the images are here, the voices are here. They are all over me, they are overwhelming, but I don't see or hear them. But not everyone is so closed. A hasidic rabbi once said that he was praying to have the voices a little bit dulled. He couldn't rest, he couldn't sleep, because he was hearing voices all the time. He was distraught from having a very broad range receiver.

Q. Is there a finer energy that can connect us to a current of life from which the call from above comes?

Steinsaltz. I have always been very, very suspicious about finding artificial means—it doesn't really matter whether it is a mantra or a drug. Do you know that book by Aldous Huxley about the gates of heaven and hell? One of his basic points (which I think was a mistake) was that he thought that somehow he had found the key to another realm. That was the basic notion, and he wrote very beautifully about it. Now, as more and more people that tried it found out, you don't get a gateway to heaven. You get, at the most, a gateway into another chamber within yourself.

Q. Isn't what we are searching for within ourselves?

Steinsaltz. No, that is not the real search. We may have wonderful experiences and clearly have within us more than we know, more than the eye catches, but we're trying to pass over and through the self to the Other. Now I may find out lots of beautiful things or horrible things within my microcosms, and there may be ways and means and exercises to get there, but the real problem is that this is still my own realm, and what I really want is to go to the Other Side. There are, I think somewhere in the United States, a few miles of receiving antennas that are meant specifically to receive calls from outer space. Just imagine that you receive such a message—you are overjoyed. You hear a voice, and it's coming from a very small transmitter on the other side of the earth. It's a wonderful discovery, but that wasn't what you were searching for. You were searching for something from the other side of nowhere. You didn't want to find something within your realm.

Q. The sound of the *shofar* in synagogue on Rosh Hashanah seems to be a call. So in a sense the call doesn't have to come from another world. There's a certain sound of another world in the *shofar*. There's a reminder in it, an awakener.

Steinsaltz. Yes, but it is like getting a beep before the news. That is what is says. It's not the news, it's just the beep telling you, I'm here tuned to the news.

Q. But at least it's a reminder.

Steinsaltz. In many ways the religious life is supposed to be a reminder. Now, as it happens, people get accustomed even to the reminder. The alarm clock is ringing and you go on sleeping. You become so accustomed to these calls that you sleep through them, and just weave them into your dream.

Q. What could be an awakener?

Steinsaltz. If I may quote the Almighty, he says in the Book of Deuteronomy: "Who will make them, or lead them, who will make them listen to Me as they are listening to Me now, that their heart will be ready for Me as it is now?" But people are not always willing to repeat this experience, because hearing such a voice is a terrible burden. It is always a shocking thing to have, so the notion of delegating it comes from a desire to protect myself from that pain, from the too-big experience. People are willing to have small adventures, small thrills, and small frights. But how many shocks can I have? Sometimes one is enough for a lifetime—I don't want to repeat it. Sometimes you have experiences that you want to repeat, but you just don't get the chance; and sometimes one is more than enough—it has been great, important, stirring, but one does not wish to go through it again. Some experiences are such that, if it is a real voice that has been heard, it is always connected and involved with either pain or very great suffering; what is called a dark, big fear is a part of it. You can see in the biblical descriptions of the prophet. It is really suffering.

Q. Are you saying that we need to suffer?

Steinsaltz. I am not speaking about the need to suffer as cleansing. I am speaking about how the experience of getting such a transmission is on its own a very painful one, and that is why people subconsciously shy away from it.

Q. At the same time—the call is maybe another word for grace, and we have the written experience of many people whose lives have been transformed by this touch from above.

Steinsaltz. Let me put it this way: There are some people who are blessed. They get a blessing, but they do not always get a call. To get a blessing is, in a certain way, a passive experience, and to hear a voice is a listening experience. This kind of listening, an active listening, demands a great effort from the listener.

Q. When *Parabola* interviewed you for the "Wholeness" issue (10:1 [1985]: 80–85), you said, "One of the first conditions is to listen. He is speaking all the time. The voice doesn't stop; we just stopped hearing. It isn't a phenomenon in time, but a phenomenon in eternity. It is our work to be ready to do the listening."

Steinsaltz. So I didn't change that much!

Q. It seems that really the most important thing for us is to listen.

Steinsaltz. To be able to listen.

Q. But how do we learn to hear?

Steinsaltz. We don't learn to hear. The only thing that we can really learn is that something may happen, and when it comes, to listen. In the first revelation to Moses, he is not sure what has happened; he has to be given some kind of sign. There's an immediate call to see a sign, the burning bush, just in order to come close, which is again the same thing: it's like knocking on the door, like feeling a hand on your shoulder. It's not in itself a message, but it is a kind of awakening. Moses hears it. The *Midrash* says that later, Moses says to God, "Reveal Yourself to me." And God says, "You cannot see My face . . . I will cover you and you will see something anyway." And the *Midrash* says that God told Moses: "When I wanted it, you didn't want it. You hid your face. When you want it, I don't want it." Sometimes the only thing to be learned is this: when the call comes, jump!

About the Author

Adin Steinsaltz, internationally regarded as one of the leading rabbis of this century, is head of the Israel Institute for Talmudic Publications. In addition to his monumental translation of and commentary on the Babylonian Talmud, Rabbi Steinsaltz is the author of many works in Hebrew and English. His series of discourses on chasidic thought contains *The Sustaining Utterance*, *The Long Shorter Way*, and *In the Beginning*. Some of his other English works include *The Strife of the Spirit*, *The Essential Talmud*, *The Thirteen Petalled Rose*, *The Tales of Rabbi Nachman of Bratslav*, and *Biblical Images*. Rabbi Steinsaltz was born and resides in Jerusalem.